GARDENING your FRONT YARD

To Rich, for your unwavering support of my creative path.

Inspiring | Educating | Creating | Entertaining

Brimming with creative inspiration, how-to projects, and useful information to enrich your everyday life, Quarto Knows is a favorite destination for those pursuing their interests and passions. Visit our site and dig deeper with our books into your area of interest: Quarto Creates, Quarto Cooks, Quarto Homes, Quarto Lives, Quarto Drives, Quarto Explores, Quarto Gifts, or Quarto Kids.

24 23 22 21 20   1 2 3 4 5

ISBN: 978-0-7603-6486-4

Digital edition published in 2020
eISBN: 978-0-7603-6487-1

Library of Congress Cataloging-in-Publication Data

Title: Gardening your front yard : projects and ideas for big and small spaces / Tara Nolan.
Description: Beverly, MA : The Quarto Group, 2020. | Includes index. | Summary: "Gardening Your Front Yard is an active, inspiring resource that shows you how to treat your front yard like a backyard without sacrificing beauty, from choosing the right plants to building front patios and walkways. With her unique combination of DIY/building savvy and gardening expertise, author Tara Nolan weaves you past the main pitfalls you may encounter when trying to fit a garden or gardens between your home and the street. This beautiful and comprehensive book shows how to accomplish several hardscape projects, such as building front patios, borders, edging, and walkways, as well as making your own raised beds, planting containers, trellises, rose arbors, privacy screens, and more-all custom-designed for the rigors of front-yard gardening"-- Provided by publisher.
Identifiers: LCCN 2019049932 | ISBN 9780760364864 (hardcover) | ISBN 9780760364871 (ebook)
Subjects: LCSH: Gardening. | Gardens--Design.
Classification: LCC SB473 .N65 2020 | DDC 635--dc23
LC record available at https://lccn.loc.gov/2019049932

Design: Burge Agency
Cover Images: Donna Griffith
Photography: see credits on photos
Illustration: Len Churchill

Printed in China

GARDENING *your* FRONT YARD

PROJECTS AND IDEAS FOR BIG & SMALL SPACES

TARA NOLAN

AUTHOR OF *RAISED BED REVOLUTION*

COOL
SPRINGS
PRESS

CONTENTS

Credit: Janis Nicolay

Credit: Star Roses & Plants

CHAPTER 1
THE FRONT YARD COMES INTO FOCUS

"Don't pick that dandelion!" my 7-year-old niece chided me one spring day as we were walking up my driveway. "That's the first source of nectar for bees in the springtime," she added—authoritatively. I love that someone had taught her that factoid—and that it stuck.

There was a time when the sight of a few dandelions would have drawn scorn from neighbors (I'm sure it still does, for some) who worried the seeds would float onto their own perfect lawns. But we have come a long way these last few years, as more and more homeowners see the value of putting their front yard gardens to better use. We have moved away from plain green lawns sprayed to eradicate any sign of other life—like dandelions—not to mention beneficial insects, which are innocent bystanders.

Walk down many urban or suburban streets these days and, chances are, you'll see at least a small mix of homes that have gone the front yard garden route—with food, flowers, or a mix of both—peppered among the traditional green lawns—both weed filled and weed free.

Many recent gardening articles have encouraged both seasoned and novice green thumbs to garden with mindfulness for the environment. Mainstream publications aren't always that overt in their messaging, but it's easy to read between the lines. All these gardening measures have a long-term goal of helping the Earth: Plant for pollinators. Plant to save the monarch butterfly. Plant to save the bees. Include drought-tolerant species to conserve water. Look for native plants at local nurseries. Capture rainwater in rain barrels to hydrate your plants. Eat local by supporting nearby small-scale farmers. Eat local by growing your own vegetables. And, to circle back to the humble dandelion, you don't have to pull all the weeds because not all weeds are bad.

These are just a few of the directives that have crept out of traditional gardening publications and into mainstream reading. Turf grass starts to look relatively useless when you apply all these ideas to your own yard and make a plan to do things such as grow food, support wildlife, and capture rainwater responsibly.

Coincidentally, while researching for this book, a few timely headlines popped up and confirmed the *zeitgeist* of this front yard shift. Within a 3-week period, the *New York Times* alone featured three lawn-averse articles: "I'm Done Mowing my Lawn: A Manicured Swath of Grass May be the Ultimate Symbol of Suburbia, but Perhaps it Shouldn't Be"; "One Thing You Can Do: Reduce Your Lawn"; and "To Nurture Nature, Neglect Your Lawn: Why Poison the Earth When You Can Have Wildflowers at Your Feet and Songbirds in Your Trees Without Even Trying?" Around the same time, *Grist*, an online nonprofit environmental magazine, didn't beat around the bush: "Lawns are the number 1 irrigated 'crop' in America. They need to die." Um, point taken! And don't even get me started on synthetic grass.

Credit: (opposite) Donna Griffith

Gardening the front yard is not a fringe concept adopted by a few forward-thinking folks. I feel as though we'll be seeing more and more innovation when it comes to front yard design and planting. And, if you think you'll miss the feeling of cool green grass between your toes on a hot summer day, look for alternative, sustainable grass varieties that require less water and maintenance.

Now is an exciting time for front yard gardens. There are just so many possibilities with purposes beyond pleasing your neighbors or potential homebuyers. In fact, the idea for this book was germinated over a discussion about how front yards are, once again, becoming social spaces. This discussion blossomed into a broader conversation about all the other modern concepts suddenly being applied to front yards, including veggies, water- and drought-driven plant choices, and cut flowers.

In my book *Raised Bed Revolution*, I was able to fit all the broader ideas together, like the pieces of a puzzle. Raised beds for big spaces? Check. Raised beds for small spaces? Check. Upcycling ideas, season extenders, and trellising options? Check, check, check. But with *Gardening Your Front Yard*, every time I crossed off a concept to include from my list, I found a new idea. I feel like the inspiration I've gathered is an unlimited mood board or scrapbook of ideas that can forever be expanded upon.

THE EVOLUTION OF CURB APPEAL

The basic goal behind curb appeal is to make your home and front yard attractive from the street—especially for potential homebuyers. It's about first impressions. Setting aside the house itself, a universally accepted aesthetic of what constitutes a desirable front yard evolved and then stayed put, frozen in time: a tidy lawn, with perhaps a tree or two, and well-manicured gardens with a mix of familiar shrubs, annuals, and perennials.

However, after being inspired to turn the front yard of my first home into a garden, I realized that curb appeal is a very individual response, much like our clothing choices or interior design. Although I thought what I'd done looked pretty good for an amateur and neighbors had commented on how much they liked it, I'm sure others grumbled to themselves about how awful it looked or worried that it was bringing down the neighborhood property values.

Since my first little foray into front yard gardening, I'm seeing more and more front yard gardens that make efficient use of the space, often with a purpose, such as cut flowers or wildflower gardens; vegetable beds; gardens to attract wildlife; eco-friendly solutions, like rain gardens; and more established patios that take front yard socializing beyond the traditional porch. Curb appeal has evolved beyond a standardized aesthetic.

In other words, the definition of curb appeal has evolved. Where it once implied the homeowner had to create a front yard garden to suit other people's tastes, both day-to-day and for potential buyers, now it has relaxed. Because if you're not planning to sell your house anytime soon, why not create a front yard garden that suits your lifestyle and your preferences?

In short, let's all agree curb appeal is in the eye of the beholder. And, sometimes, the point of view is from inside looking out.

LET THE BRAINSTORMING BEGIN

For this book, I drew from a variety of sources and inspiration. I tapped into other people's imaginations and found that the process sparked fresh ideas of my own. I knocked on a few doors in my town to see if I could get permission to photograph the owners' gardens. I consulted experts, some of whom I've never met, but follow on social media (most likely Instagram). I even delved into some of my past travels, including the 2017 Royal Horticultural Society Chelsea Flower Show, where a handful of British garden designers made an indelible impression.

A front yard garden, like any garden, evolves. Although it's easy to get excited about all the possibilities, it's also easy to become overwhelmed by the mammoth task of overhauling a property, whether it's the size of a postage stamp or a hobby farm. Whether you're working from your own design or plan or one that's been drawn up by a professional, don't think you have to complete the project all at once. Choose a chunk of your vision to work on each season, such as laying down cardboard to smother grass in the fall so an area is ready for planting come spring. Then, slowly build on it over time.

Tiered hedges add depth to a small front yard garden.
Credit: Donna Griffith

When it comes to my front yard garden, I'm playing the long game of chipping away at it bit by bit. I started out (very) slowly, rather than ripping out huge swaths of sod. The first step in expanding my front garden into my current lawn involved widening the garden and then taking out a band of grass at the foot of it. I haven't completely finished planting the whole garden yet, but each season I add perennials and other plants to fill in the spaces. I can't wait to see it finished, but I must be patient and remind myself that, eventually, it will all come together.

I've divided this book into chapters, but, really, you could incorporate ideas from each to create a sustainable garden that will spark conversations with passersby and help further the vision of what a front yard garden can be.

THE NITTY-GRITTY REALITIES OF FRONT-YARD GARDENING

When I ripped apart my first front yard, turning grass into garden, I didn't know what I was doing. It was such a tiny space and, luckily, it turned out well—although I'm sure I would have benefitted from professional suggestions. There are, in fact, some aspects of gardening and lawn care for which consulting a professional can save you from costly mistakes. For example, you should call a professional when you're dealing with anything that will change the grade or slope of the property. You don't want to inadvertently divert water from a wet spot you didn't realize was there toward, say, your foundation or a neighbor's property. You should also be aware of where underground lines and pipes are located.

The "off season" presents the perfect opportunity to gather ideas, sketch, plan—and figure out if your budget can accommodate everything on your wish list!

There's something to be said about getting out and seeing gardens in person. Take a walk through different neighborhoods where you live. One house might not have the entire front yard garden that you're dreaming of, but their space may contain elements you want to incorporate into your personalized design.

Check your local newspaper listings for garden tours. I am surrounded by garden clubs and horticultural societies, and they all offer garden tours each year. There's even an event called Open Garden Week in my area, where homeowners open their gardens to the public at certain times and you can just walk right in. Often you get to speak to the homeowners, which is nice because they can help when it comes to sourcing that gorgeous plant that just caught your eye, those fabulous pots for container gardening, or some interesting hardscaping materials.

South of me, across the border, Garden Walk Buffalo, America's largest garden tour, takes place over a weekend every July and features more than 400 gardens you can visit at your leisure. Home gardens range from the traditional to downright quirky, but all offer a treasure trove of ideas you can take home to your garden.

So, do a little "digging" and see what your community and surrounding towns and cities offer for prospective green thumbs throughout spring and summer. It just might be worth a day trip or an overnight excursion to gather inspiration.

FRONT YARD GARDEN INSPIRATION

As a starting point into your front yard garden exploration, here are some inspiring homes and gardens that may just spark an idea you can apply to your space.

Consider monochromatic plantings. This study in green contrast nicely with the light paint color of the home. Credit: Roger Yip

A small front yard garden can be planted in carefully shaped layers to appear lush and full. Credit: Roger Yip

Sometimes, the house itself contributes to the beauty of a garden. This one features low-maintenance perennials, such as ornamental grasses, and a dry creek bed, a.k.a. a rain garden, which diverts rain away from the house and hydrates the plants around it. Credit: Donna Griffith

Learn about how rain filters into dry creek beds in front yard gardens in chapter 5, which features eco-friendly garden design ideas.
Credit: Donna Griffith

This front yard garden is, essentially, a miniature "field" of lavender with other perennials interplanted among the fragrant stems. The largest grouping besides the lavender is two types of thyme. Passersby will also discover orange and white day lilies, poppies, daisies, various types of stonecrop, and hens and chicks. Plants that can tolerate full sun and little watering were deliberately chosen for this lush, fragrant, densely planted garden.
Credit: Donna Griffith

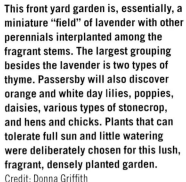

If you want to tuck a few veggies into your front yard garden, but aren't ready to dig up a full garden bed (or don't have the space!), consider gardening in a container, like this self-watering Vegepod, which can fit a generous amount of plants. Credit: Vegepod Australia

It may not have a lawn, but grass is still the predominant plant in this arid front garden. Many ornamental grasses are drought resistant, making them great low-maintenance options.
Credit: Jim Charlier

This above-par idea wins points for being clever *and* gorgeous. Homeowner Brent Warriner is a lifelong golf enthusiast. How perfect is it that he ended up with a house number that just happens to be the same as the number of holes on a regular golf course? "I was bored with maintaining a pristine lawn, so I wanted to try something fun, creative, and different," he explains. Brent consulted with a landscape architect and worked with landscapers and other professionals to bring his vision to life.

Each grass or groundcover has been carefully chosen to play into the golf theme in this garden. "I used two kinds of blue fescue instead of green grass, so people didn't think my lawn was overgrown weeds," he says.

As Brent explains it, the short blue fescue is the putting green/collar. The long blue fescue is the fairway/rough. The black grass (not pictured) is the water from the penalty area. The yellow groundcover is two bunkers. There is a teeing area on the other side of the driveway (not shown) with a big swath of grass representing the swinging golfer. The magnolia is Brent's landscaping connection to the Augusta National Golf Club, and the rock border is from Manitoulin Island, Ontario, which is reminiscent of golfing in the Canadian Shield. A couple of props (a flag marking a golf "hole" and two tee markers) are not shown. The Adirondack/Muskoka chairs were a last-minute decision for Brent's wife, Karen, who likes to chat with the neighbors while the kids play. Credit: Donna Griffith

According to garden designer Candy Venning, the shady front garden of this historic home was nothing but dust. Elements of the home are reflected in the design—the brickwork reflects the home's stonework, whereas the iron fence mimics the arch of the window.
Credit: Candy Venning

In the 31 years of being in the wildflower seed business, Paul Jenkins of Wildflower Farm says thousands of homeowners have sown meadows in their front yards. Credit: wildflowerfarm.com

While you might not want to get rid of all of your lawn, there are creative ways to design a bigger garden bed that eliminates some of it. Credit: Karin Banerd

Steven Biggs started his front yard garden project as an edible-themed garden, with small fruit, edible flowers, and vegetables. He did this to make a statement after there was some opposition to a nearby community vegetable garden. Bit by bit, Steven has been adding nonedibles to his front yard garden. When his mom passed away a few years ago, he started adding more flowers to remember her. They're planted among the Nanking cherry, Saskatoon and Haskap berries, hosta spears and daylilies (both edible), cardoon, and nasturtiums. Credit: Steven Biggs

What's your garden style? Cottage gardens work well in small spaces (and with small, quaint homes), where sprawling and climbing blooms cast their magic in a riot of color. Credit: The Complete Guide to Landscape Projects

When figuring out the design of your front yard garden, consider interesting shapes that feature both in-ground plantings and pots. Credit: The Complete Guide to Landscape Projects

HIRING A LANDSCAPE PROFESSIONAL

In which instances should your green thumb dial (or email) a landscape professional? This completely depends on your individual needs. If you're overhauling or renovating your property, some expert advice will help guide your decisions and raise points or opportunities you might not have considered. But, if you find yourself owning a new house with a well-established garden, you have a good eye, and you just want to make your own mark with minor cosmetic changes, go for it alone.

If you want to overhaul or renovate your property on a grander scale—or even if you just need someone to make recommendations about plants and how to arrange them—expert advice will guide your decisions and bring up points you might not have thought of, such as checking for placement of underground utilities.

Consider hiring a landscape professional as a consultant, someone who can draw up a plan that you can then chip away at on your own over time. If there is some major earth moving or hardscaping involved, your consultant can organize the project, hire the appropriate tradespeople, and see you through the construction process. Either way, you'll gain valuable expertise.

A good way to find a landscape professional is through recommendations from friends or family. Reach out to your network for photos and gather testimonials that will help you decide whom to hire. Here are some reasons a professional may be the one to help you realize your gardening dreams:

Training and experience

The person you hire has a degree in or has taken courses relating to the field. Ask to see samples of their work. If possible, get permission to visit some of the gardens they have completed. The expert will be able to guide you through the process, identify your likes and dislikes, and be frank about whether your ideas are realistic. For example, what you have in mind may require lots of maintenance you don't have time for. A professional will steer you toward a plan that works with your lifestyle.

Design vision

The landscape professional you hire should be passionate about gardening. A creative, artistic professional views each garden as a canvas, ready to be "painted." Don't be afraid to share your ideas—they will be happy to incorporate those into the plan. The expert you hire will be able to help you define your style and will ask you questions to help them determine the style that best represents you. A landscape designer will take all ideas and work them into what they feel is the best solution for the space and the client. They'll also take into consideration the look of your home, so the garden style blends seamlessly with the exterior features.

Access to trusted tradespeople

The person you hire should be able to call upon a network of associates who can work on various elements of the project, from earth moving to hardscaping to carpentry. They'll know if there are permits you need to get to launch a bigger front yard garden project. They'll be familiar with local regulations or bylaws that might impact your ideas. Furthermore, if you don't have the tools or equipment or even someone in your family to do the heaving lifting, having the work done for you can save time, energy, and maybe even money.

Melanie Wynne lives in the sunny, hot northern end of Sonoma County, where it only rains from late October to late March. Based on her garden's conditions, she designed small, repetitive garden groupings that can withstand direct sun, use small amounts of water, and included both rocks from her backyard and zone-appropriate plants that are both deer-resistant and pollinator-friendly. Credit: Melanie Wynne

Increase the value of your home

Curb appeal can be a big deal to homeowners. Many sources recommend spending about 10 percent of your home's value on landscaping. Even spreading a tidy layer of mulch around some nice perennials can elevate the look of your front yard garden.

Project management and time

A professional will be able to create a workback plan with deadlines, so you know when various stages of work will be complete, not to mention the final garden.

Budget

A landscape professional will take your budget seriously and formulate a plan accordingly. This may mean breaking up the project into phases to accommodate your budget, if it can't cover everything at once. The professional you hire will have established contacts in the trades to oversee various parts of the project. And, they'll likely have access to and knowledge of wholesale pricing for plants and materials you may not find at a local garden center.

Plant knowledge

Landscape designers tend to be plant enthusiasts. "We can match plants to soil and exposure better than most folks can because we've tried and failed, and we've taken the time to develop those skills," explains landscape designer Sean James. Sourcing plants is another bonus—a landscape designer may have access to or knowledge of where they can get more unusual plant varieties.

STAGING YOUR GARDEN FOR CURB APPEAL

In speaking to landscape professionals for this book, I was alerted to the correlation between ROI (return on investment) of front yard gardens and JOY scores (a calculation of the happiness and satisfaction homeowners reported for their renovation projects) by garden designer Karin Banerd of Garden by Design. Karin provided the following thoughts on the topic.

If resale value is top of mind because you may be selling your home imminently, there are a few factors you may want to consider. Karin points out that the front yard outranks both kitchen and bathroom redos for ROI.

"Decluttering and rearranging furniture inside a home will enhance its appearance and saleability, but uncluttering the exterior and rearranging some plants may be even more important," she explains. "The right choices can make a home look bigger, more spacious, and organized (similar to the goals of interior home staging)."

According to the National Association of Realtors, even a minor landscaping upgrade, such as a planter, flagstone pathway, or a few flowering shrubs and a small tree, provides an average return exceeding 100 percent. Even edging and mulching the garden can do wonders to the front yard's overall appearance.

And, if you happen to be staying put with your new front yard garden? A report put out by the National Association of Realtors and the National Association of Landscape Professionals stated that an overall landscape upgrade received a JOY Score of 9.8 (with 10 being the highest score) and an ROI of just over 100 percent.

MEASURE YOUR GARDEN'S CONDITIONS

When you move into a new home, it takes a while to get to know your property. Although you look at it every day, it's likely there are things you don't think about, like where runoff water collects, which trees cast the most shade, and the sun's position at key points throughout the day. These last two points will help you figure out what to plant where—from full shade to full sun. If you're planting vegetables—tomatoes, cucumbers, and squash, for example—your space needs to get at least six to eight hours of sun per day.

To assess how much sun your front yard gets, make a rough sketch of the garden. Record where the light hits the yard every two hours throughout the day. If you have any trees shading the property, do this exercise once the trees have leafed out in spring. Your light conditions will be very different throughout the year.

PLANTING AROUND A FOUNDATION

Most homes have gardens around the foundation to soften and frame the point where the house meets the ground, as opposed to just seeing a box of bricks plunked onto the earth. This type of planting even has its own name: foundation planting. However, there are some things to be mindful of when planting close to your home.

If you have a completely blank slate, consider having a professional draw up a design based on your gardening style. Or, take a crack at drawing your own plan!

Don't mound up the soil any higher than it already is—you want to be able to see a bit of your foundation for regular inspections. And make sure that, if there is any slope, it flows away from the house.

Be aware of where utility pipes come out of the house.

Leave at least 1' (0.3 m) of space between your house and where a mature plant's width will eventually reach. This will promote air circulation and prevent rotting as well as help prevent roots from growing into the foundation.

Stick to shrubs, as a tree's root system can extend one to two times beyond the height of the tree. Consider choosing compact varieties.

Read plant tags carefully to see how tall and wide a tree or shrub will become as it matures. Depending on the size of your home, you might want to consider dwarf or compact varieties. Maintain a regular pruning schedule to prevent your tree or shrub from becoming unmanageable.

Add a layer of mulch to the garden to conserve moisture.

Leave at least 1' (0.3 m) of space between your house and the likely mature width of your foundation plantings. Credit: Donna Griffith

BYLAWS, BONUSES, AND SOIL

Many counties, townships, and municipalities have specific bylaws in place that dictate what can be done to a property's landscape. Often, these are directed specifically at boulevards and pertain to setbacks and plant height. Research the rules that govern the area where you live and proceed accordingly.

Check for municipality bonuses.

Does your city or township have any gardening programs in place that green thumbs can take advantage of? Check to see if your local governments offer initiatives, such as rain barrel sales, free tree planting programs, free compost and mulch giveaways, and so on.

Dealing with soil: amendments for new builds, compost, and more.

If you move into a house with healthy, friable soil, consider yourself very lucky. However, don't think you can rest on your bay laurels. It's up to you to continue to work on your property's soil health each year.

The area around new a house's foundation is filled in with anything available, so the soil might not be the healthiest. But it's possible to improve it. Be patient and remember it will take time to build up healthy soil. Good compost is your friend. If you don't have your own compost pile, that's okay. You can order a big load in spring to be delivered, or you can rely on the bags of compost you see each spring at the garden center. Shrimp, mushroom, manure, and organic vegetable compost are just some of the labels you'll see.

In fall, take advantage of the leaves—free compost! Gently run over them with your lawnmower so they are shredded into smaller bits and sprinkle them in your gardens where they'll break down over winter.

Foundation plantings soften the transition between your house and lawn or gardens. Choose relatively compact varieties with some color and four-season interest.
Credit: Shutterstock

For a larger home, you can think bigger, while keeping in mind foundation planting rules.
Credit: Nick McCullough

GETTING RID OF GRASS WITH CARDBOARD

I recommend cardboard to gardeners who want to get rid of grass so they can install raised beds and pathways. This process is a little easier when you're dealing with a smaller space—mostly because it's likely out of sight. When you're dealing with your front yard, your intentions are public. Whether you want to tackle a whole area at once or perhaps choose small sections, if that's an option, add a layer of cardboard on top of the grass you'd like to smother and cover it with soil. Over time, the cardboard will break down the grass, leaving fresh soil in its place. The best time to do this is in fall so you have the entire winter for the grass to decompose.

Garden writer Donna Balzer used cardboard with a layer of mulch over top to smother the grass in her front yard and then turned it all into garden and a big front yard patio. Credit: Donna Balzer

DIGGING UP SOD

If you wish to re-lay your healthy turfgrass elsewhere in your yard, a rented sod stripper (also known as a sod cutter) does a neat, professional job of removing sod. Gas-powered models may be available, too, for bigger areas.
Credit: The Complete Outdoor Builder

CALL BEFORE YOU DIG

For most big gardening projects, including digging up sod, planting a tree, or otherwise digging deeply into the soil, you'll need to know if there are gas lines or other utility lines lurking in the front yard that could be damaged by a shovel—and dangerous to the gardener.

In the United States, 811 is the number to call. In Canada and elsewhere, consult your gas company and/or your local municipality.

Even after grubs had decimated our lawn in my first home, it was very time-consuming to dig up big rectangles of dead sod. Furthermore, our municipality did not accept loose pieces of sod in the paper compost bags we put on the curb (probably because of the weight), so we had to figure out what to do with it.

But, if you do decide to pull up grass, measure the area you'd like to eliminate. Use an edger or a sharp square spade to slice the sod into pieces. Dig it out and dispose of it accordingly.

Your sod might come in handy in other areas of your property. For example, one thing you can do with pieces of sod is turn it upside-down, soil-side up, and use it to fill a raised bed.

REDUCING NOISE AND ADDRESSING SECURITY CONCERNS IN YOUR FRONT YARD GARDEN

T rees and shrubs are not very effective when it comes to blocking noise, but they can, at least, create a feeling of privacy, insulation, and coziness—especially when they are fully leafed out. They may be used to shield a front yard garden from a busy street. Another way to reduce noise can be to introduce your own soothing sounds, for example with a water fountain, to counterbalance traffic noise or loud neighbors.

As a security precaution, you don't want anything to block sight lines to the front door and windows from the street, so shrubs should only be about 3' (0.9 m) tall in those areas. In general, don't create hiding places for would-be intruders to conceal themselves.

Other security considerations can be as simple as a locked gate that prevents anyone from easily getting into the backyard where they're out of sight from the road. Picket fences and spiny plants, such as roses and barberry, can be used as deterrents around the periphery of your property, though you should also keep them fairly low.

Lighting is another element you can add, particularly motion sensor-activated lights, to illuminate any suspicious activity.

Other things you might want to do include securing bigger items, such as benches or urns, with chains or bolts (that likely can be concealed) if outdoor décor in your neighborhood seems to go missing.

This front yard garden, which leads to two apartments with separate entrances, features a security gate at sidewalk level to enter the premises. Credit: Tracey Ayton

TAKING YOUR GARDEN WITH YOU

L ooking to move? Talk to your real estate agent about any clauses you'd like to include in your sales contract that explain what you'd like to take with you, such as any perennial plants. You can't leave the new owners with holes in the ground without warning them first! Though sometimes it is nice to start fresh, I do wish I had done something like that when selling our first home. The house ended up being torn down to build a bigger one and all those gorgeous, established perennials were removed for good.

WHAT TOOLS DO I NEED?

Not everyone has a giant tool collection. If your project requires an item you don't own and you can't borrow it from a friend or neighbor, see if there are local companies or a big-box store where you can rent the tools you need. Some cities even have tool lending libraries that you join as you would a regular library (though there may be a small fee) and sign out tools as you need them.

The gardening and yard tools you're likely to use the most are relatively common and inexpensive. Credit: Shutterstock

SLOPE STYLE: DEALING WITH PROPERTIES THAT HAVE AN INCLINE

If your home is perched on a slope, you might either have a really steep lawn that's hard to cut or a garden that's not very accessible to weed, water, and plant. However, working to overhaul a slope can be tricky business. If you move into a home with a steep incline and want to do anything to it besides working with the existing conditions, this is where a landscape professional's expert opinion would be extremely valuable.

There are key factors that need to be considered when you're changing the grade of the property in any way. Water runoff is a big one: Water has to have a place to go— you don't want to inadvertently alter the property in a way that will negatively affect your home or an adjacent neighbor's home.

Terracing and retaining walls are common solutions to dealing with a slope. They can help ease the steep angle, while presenting an easier, flat space in which to garden— and you'll get more light exposure for your plants by gardening on different levels. A retaining wall will cut into the slope, bridging a predetermined upper and lower level.

It's recommended that, if building your own retaining wall, you go no higher than 3' (0.9 m). Anything greater should be handled by a landscape professional who will be able to address the structural integrity of the project and build accordingly.

If you are undertaking an exceptionally big project (not just a few stones added to a small garden to create a terrace), you may also need to look into whether you need a permit.

In my first home, there was a very gradual, shallow slope leading away from the front of the house, so my husband and I were able to build a very low retaining wall out of stone to create a level, terraced garden, rather than trying to garden on the slope itself. That was an easy weekend DIY project.

In my current home, I'd like to terrace part of the lawn bordering the driveway. It's a bit of a dry, steep, exposed slope where grass doesn't grow quite as thickly (in fact in a hot summer, it goes dormant completely), and it's also challenging to mow. Putting a garden in its place would allow me to plant a selection of drought-tolerant perennials—

and sneak in a few edibles—because it's a prime, full-sun spot for heat lovers, such as tomatoes and peppers. For this project, I'd consult a professional.

If you'd like to add a four-sided raised bed garden to a slope, please refer to chapter 4 on growing veggies in front yards for detailed instructions.

This home, with its steep front slope, was a labor of love worked on for 20 years by the couple who live here. There is even a "garden room" nestled atop the garage "roof," with a patio table and umbrella, barely visible from the street. Credit: Leslie O'Connell

This gorgeous garden sits atop a sizeable terrace surrounded by a lush, beautiful garden providing privacy from the street below.
Credit: Tracey Ayton

A limestone retaining wall creates garden levels, making it easier to maintain the perennial planting.
Credit: The Complete Guide to Landscape Projects

CHAPTER 2
FRONT YARD LIVING:
A RETURN TO BEING SOCIAL IN THE FRONT YARD

I grew up in a subdivision where the homes were spaced rather far apart and set back from the road. But my husband, who grew up in an urban neighborhood with houses built more closely together, remembers his parents and neighbors socializing on hot summer nights on one of their front porches, while the kids roamed the neighborhood playing.

At some point over the years, everyone retreated to their backyards. Don't get me wrong: I love my backyard and the privacy it provides. I like the fact I can eat my breakfast on my deck in my pajamas and only the birds and squirrels can see me. But there is something really nice about getting to know the people who live on my street. A few of my neighbors can be found on their front porches on mild evenings. And when I'm out gardening, neighbors walking by will often stop to chat —or pull their cars over to say hello. Gardening may be solitary when you're doing the work, but it's inherently social if you encounter a fellow green thumb who is interested in what you are planting and doing.

A very recent article in Minnesota's *Star Tribune* newspaper carried the subtitle, "A wave of front yard patios spurs socializing on one convivial block in St. Louis Park." One of the homeowners interviewed said they'll retreat to the backyard to relax or barbecue dinner, but the front is where they head when they're feeling more social.

Once I read this article, I started to notice the odd front yard patio on my walks. One home I walk past has four comfy chairs arranged around an outdoor fire pit. It's simple and classy, and I can imagine the owners kicking back to relax after a long day at work—though I haven't caught them out there yet.

There's certainly a way to nicely integrate a patio into your front yard. Of course, if you already have a front porch, you're set. I dream of a home with a lovely covered front porch where I can cuddle up under a blanket in a rainstorm or chat with friends over summer drinks. But, for now, I have an oddly placed concrete area that I decided to dress up a bit, the main items being my outdoor Adirondack/Muskoka chairs and, of course, plants.

On Bluezones.com, a website with the aim to help people live longer, better lives by improving their environments, there is an article entitled "Happiness Lessons from Around the World." One of the happiness lessons is to choose the front porch over the back deck because of the potential to socialize. Unless your neighbors are especially grumpy or nosy, make an effort to get to know them. Apparently, this can add to your overall happiness.

Credit: (opposite) ShawnaCoronado.com

This is my front yard seating area. It took a few years to decide on the blue stain to preserve the cedar Adirondack/Muskoka chairs (the names vary according to where you live: Adirondack is common in the United States). I'm not particularly fond of all the concrete surrounding my house but I wanted to jazz up this little seating nook, so I included an outdoor carpet to add color and hide some of it. It's funny how a coat of paint on those chairs made me want to sit in them more. I'm out there all the time now.
Credit: Donna Griffith

When asked why he added a bench to his garden, horticulturist Spencer Hauck said that it was placed there for both social reasons and to rest. He says his mailman always took a break in the garden, so, when he designed the current garden, he added a walkway and bench offering the option to sit and enjoy the view. Spencer also enjoys sitting out there to work. Credit: Spencer Hauck

The chairs on your front porch don't have to be for show. Make sure you sit in them to relax and admire your garden—and even have the odd neighbor over for a chat. Credit: Shutterstock

ADDING A PATIO TO YOUR GARDEN

Front yard patios aren't really new but, traditionally, they were set on a porch. Who doesn't dream of that wraparound porch where you can lounge in the shade on a chaise and catch a soft breeze on a hot summer day while sipping lemonade? This is the traditional and historically acceptable vision of front yard living, right? But you don't often see the seating area find its way off the porch, built into a "garden room." That's usually a concept reserved for the backyard.

Except there's no reason that having a seating area cannot be applied to the front yard, too, depending on your lifestyle. Maybe you are a busy parent who'd like to have a spot to sit with other moms and dads while your kids play. Or, you have visions of neighbors coming by at cocktail hour to enjoy the front yard. Or, you simply need a place to rest with a glass of water between all that bending and kneeling in the garden. Whatever your purpose for front yard garden seating, there are a few considerations to think about.

First, do you want the area to be public or private? If you don't have the luxury of distance from the street or sidewalk but you want privacy, you'll need to figure out how to surround your space with plants to create a private little nook. Otherwise, it's pretty easy to create a more open space if you're open to chitchat from passersby.

Back to the idea of a garden "room," the trick is to figure out a way to integrate a seating area seamlessly into your space.

Depending on where you live, anchoring the furniture somehow to prevent it from being stolen may be a needed step.

A COZY FRONT YARD RETREAT

The purpose of Stephanie Rose's front yard garden is to create a buffer between the busy sidewalk and the front entrance to her home. As a founder of the gorgeous, idea-laden website Garden Therapy, it occurred to Stephanie that, because she doesn't spend much time in the front garden, she doesn't think of creating projects for it.

But then she realized the one thing that the space lacked was a place to actually enjoy the garden. "Looking at the garden in a new light helped me see what the space could become," she explained. So a bench was added (see photo on the right), followed by a welcoming fountain where she says she can sit and sip coffee while watching the bees enjoy the water.

Credit: Stephanie Rose

BOOKS, BLOOMS, AND A BENCH

In front of this urban home, at the edge of its front yard garden, sits a Little Free Library with a welcoming bench attached. Homeowner, Maryanne, and her partner, Bill, are both voracious readers who have always loved the idea of outdoor libraries. "Even as a child, I used to play librarian and had a check-in/check-out system for my kids' books," says Maryanne. "We wanted to do something nice for our wonderful neighborhood, so Bill designed something special. The steel reflects a design in our back garden area and is an homage to Steel Town [a moniker for the city where the couple live]. My best friend, Jeff, who is a gifted carpenter and cabinetmaker, built and stained the actual library box, and I am the librarian. The decision for the placement was deliberate as well, so people could actually sit within the front of the garden."

When asked if she catches people sitting on the bench, Maryanne replies that yes, she sees older folks sitting for a "rest," before carrying on with their walks. She says some people will ask if it's okay first. "One late night a few years ago, we saw a young man in a meditative pose, just quietly sitting—it would have made a great photo," she adds. Anyone who sits on the library's bench, depending on the time of year, can enjoy the fresh scent of lavender wafting from the garden.

Credit: Donna Griffith

TURNING GRASS INTO A GARDEN

This new front yard garden was designed to be more accessible (several shallow stairs instead of one long run of steep stairs), easier to look after, water efficient, fun to sit in and enjoy in the evening, and a great source of interesting edible and ornamental plants. Credit: Donna Balzer

G arden writer Donna Balzer's motivation for turning grass into garden and patio was, as she describes it, finally facing reality. "We live in a climate with rain in winter and a very dry summer, so, unless we really worked at it, the lawn was always dead from May to September," she explains. Meanwhile, the fringe of green just kept growing and blooming. And so, cardboard and mulch were laid to eliminate the last of the grass.

With a little view of the ocean from the front yard, Donna wanted to keep everything pretty low, leaving the existing shrubs, but with no new trees added. Challenges included the extreme heat, which required heat- and drought-tolerant plants, as well as the many hungry deer in the neighborhood.

Donna discovered the deer don't seem to touch *Salvia* (but it attracts hummingbirds), watermelons (at the grandkids' request), and snapdragons. Globe artichokes provide texture and color, with the added bonus of being edible. "When we started planting them along our side boulevard, people stopped to ask about them all the time," says Donna. "So we just had to use them again."

Last, but not least, hardscaping made the space more accessible (steep stairs were replaced with more shallow steps), and required less maintenance.

KEEPING AN EYE ON THE KIDS IN STYLE

This home is located on a dead-end street, so the kids tend to play in the front yards because there's not much traffic. The homeowners found they were in the front yard all the time so they could see the kids playing. So, they decided that's where they wanted to make the garden and where they wanted to be instead of the backyard. Credit: Donna Griffith

A PLACE TO BE SOCIAL—AND SUPERVISE

These Adirondack/Muskoka chairs were last-minute additions to this front yard garden. Homeowner Karen Beattie, whose husband, Brent, chose the garden's plants to resemble elements of a golf course, wanted a place to catch up with neighbors and watch the kids play. Credit: Donna Griffith

PATIO SET MAKEOVER

PHOTOS BY DONNA GRIFFITH
PAINT AND LACQUER PROVIDED
BY ANNIE SLOAN INTERIORS LTD.

TOOLS

Metal wire scrub brush (optional)

Paint brush

Drop cloth

Can opener (for the paint cans)

Plastic dish for paint

Eye protection

Gloves

MATERIALS

Outdoor paint

Outdoor lacquer

Do you enjoy hosting afternoon tea in your front garden? Why not? This wrought iron café set may have looked a little worse for wear from sitting outside over the years, but it was in perfect condition. Really, it just needed a refresh.

Instead of kicking old outdoor furniture to the curb, consider giving it a makeover. If a piece is broken, see if it's something you or an expert can fix to keep it out of the landfill. If you don't have anything to turn into your next DIY and you're not in the market to purchase a brand-new set, pop into local antiques markets, estate sales, and yard sales to see if you can find a rough gem you can polish into a garden treasure. It's amazing what a coat of paint and some TLC can do.

REFINISHING YOUR FURNITURE

Spread out your drop cloth. Paint the furniture following the paint manufacturer's directions and allow it to dry completely between coats. Add a coat of outdoor lacquer if you are not using an enamel paint.

THE FUN DIY PART

If you want to try to remove any paint on your project (although many outdoor products can be applied directly over old paint), use a metal wire scrub brush to remove the paint. You can either use a handheld brush or a wire wheel attachment for a portable drill. Wear eye protection when using wire brushes. Clean the furniture and allow it to dry thoroughly before painting.

Choose your paint product. I have long admired the different looks you can achieve on furniture using Chalk Paint invented by Annie Sloan. For this project, I used Chalk Paint in English Yellow and covered it with a Chalk Paint Lacquer (a water-based polyacrylic varnish with UV protection) in matte.

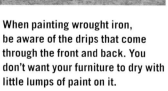

When painting wrought iron, be aware of the drips that come through the front and back. You don't want your furniture to dry with little lumps of paint on it.

This lacquer, meant for outdoor furniture and other exterior surfaces, offers UV protection to prevent fading and also creates an easy-to-clean finish.

RUSTIC LIVE-EDGE BENCH

DESIGNED AND BUILT BY MARCEL CAMPOSILVAN
PHOTOS BY DONNA GRIFFITH
ILLUSTRATION BY LEN CHURCHILL

TOOLS

Straightedge or chalk line

Square

Circular saw

Drill

Orbital sander

Paintbrush

Eye protection

MATERIALS

Two 6' (1.8 m) pieces live-edge wood

Ten or twelve 3$\frac{1}{2}$" (8.9 cm) Torx head structural lag screws

Oil finish (this project used Behr Premium Transparent Penetrating Oil Wood Finish)

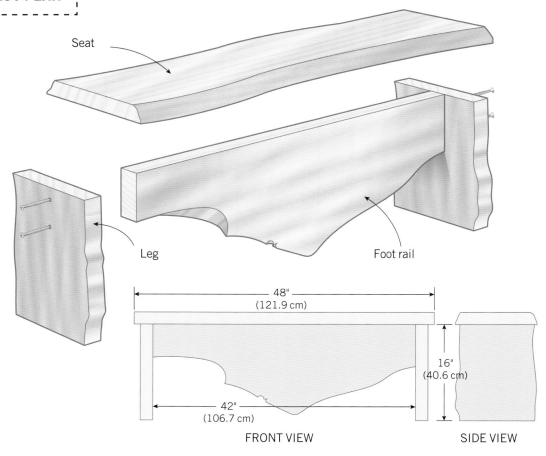

Seat

Leg

Foot rail

48"
(121.9 cm)

42"
(106.7 cm)

16"
(40.6 cm)

FRONT VIEW

SIDE VIEW

Most gardeners will complain they are far too busy planting, pruning, weeding, watering, and maintaining to find enough time to enjoy their garden. But everyone needs a break now and then—even from our hobbies. What better way to enjoy what's been planted, what's in bloom, and to see your garden from a fresh angle than by taking a moment to pause, sit, relax, and look around?

If space permits, the purpose of having a seating area in your front garden can be either social or reflective, or perhaps both. If neighbors like to happen by and discuss the garden, this bench can provide a nice place to rest and have a gab. If your front yard garden affords a bit of privacy, the bench can be placed in a more obscure spot where you can enjoy the space you've created in solitude.

The creator of this particular bench, professional carpenter Marcel Camposilvan, dubbed it "the 15-minute bench." Although it might take others longer to measure and cut and piece things together, I do think this project has a simplicity to it that even a novice carpenter could tackle.

The bench is built using a live-edge piece of wood. A live edge means the original edge, bark and all, plus the original shape, are part of the piece, rather than it being milled to, say, a perfect 2 × 4' (0.6 × 1.2 m) piece with uniform, straight edges. The live edge adds character to both indoor and outdoor furniture.

THAT FUNKY
FOOT RAIL SHAPE

Bench designer Marcel Camposilvan said he kept the shape of the foot rail for visual interest. "There was a crotch in the wood slabs, which is the area between two branches. As the tree grows, the grain inside can create this 'curly' effect. I did have to square off the top with a straightedge. I ripped off the straighter side of the live edge to cut the square ends to reinforce the legs. Also, ripping off the straighter part of the live edge was easier," he explains.

The foot rail also acts as a support beam, preventing sag of the seating and strengthening the legs to avoid wobbling.

Live-edge lumber has become pretty easy to source. A quick Google search of your area should yield results either through a company or via a classified listing.

For this bench, the rustic look of the live edge blends well into the landscape. And, in this instance, the interesting curve of the wood was used to create the foot rail (the piece that extends from leg to leg, underneath the seat, stabilizing the bench).

Nestle your new garden addition among a swath of flowers in a cottage garden, or set it in a blank space just waiting for the perfect perennial plant. This alternative might be the perfect perennial object to add to your front yard garden, among the flowers and foliage.

Thinking outside the front yard, this bench would also make a lovely addition to a community or public garden or in a big front entryway inside or out, where you sit on it and pull on your gardening shoes. Or, just put it to work as a fancy shelf for displaying flowerpots or even stashing garden supplies.

PUTTING IT TOGETHER

Note: Because no two live edges are alike, your bench's appearance and dimensions will likely differ somewhat from the one shown.

---

1. Cut 2 legs, one from each piece of live edge wood, each measuring 16" (40.6 cm) long. The legs are cut making sure they are parallel at each end, as they may not be "square" to the live edge.

---

2. Cut the seat from one of the leftover ends to 48" (1.2 m) and the foot rail from the other leftover end to 42" (1.1 m). All pieces retain their width (10 to 18" [25.4 to 45.7 cm]).

---

3. Use the lag screws to attach the foot rail to the legs, and then to the seat. Modern "ledger-style" lag screws are narrow, with high tensile strength, and, best of all, self-tapping, so no pilot holes are needed. If your live edge is hardwood, you may need to predrill the holes.

Sand the top and sides of your project using a random orbit sander.

After wiping off the sawdust left by the sander, paint on a protective finish to preserve the wood. The one applied here adds UV protection from the sun and is mildew resistant. If the species of wood you have chosen is naturally weather resistant, such as cedar or redwood, you can also leave the bench without a finish and let it weather to a natural gray.

VERTICAL PRIVACY PLANT STAND

DESIGNED AND BUILT BY JAMIE GILGEN OF CADENCE FURNITURE
PHOTOS BY DONNA GRIFFITH
ILLUSTRATION BY LEN CHURCHILL

TOOLS

Tape measure

Very sharp pencil or, better yet, marking knife

Saw (jigsaw, power miter saw, or hand saw)

Wood chisel

Mallet for chisel work

Drill and ½" (1.3 cm) to 1" (2.5 cm) wood bit

³⁄₈" (1 cm) dowel and ³⁄₈" (1 cm) drill bit

Router

Eye protection

MATERIALS

1 piece of 2 × 2" × 8' (5 × 5 cm × 2.4 m) outdoor lumber tor the pole

5' (1.5 m) of 10" (25.4 cm) deckboards for 20" (51 cm) shelves and plinths

Having a bit of privacy doesn't have to mean building a fence or a creating a full, permanent, or semipermanent, barrier. There are ways to obscure a space and enable a bit of privacy, while still allowing light and a little breeze to pass through. I've seen lightweight curtains blowing gently in the wind along the side of a porch, as well as bamboo screens that can be pulled up or down to protect a seating area from the sun.

This vertical plant stand uses strategically placed flowerpots to provide a bit of privacy from the street on a small front porch. It could be modified to fit other places, such as along a deck. Imagine a grouping of three along the side of a pergola. This project also presents a pretty vertical garden if there is not a lot of space in the front yard for a garden bed.

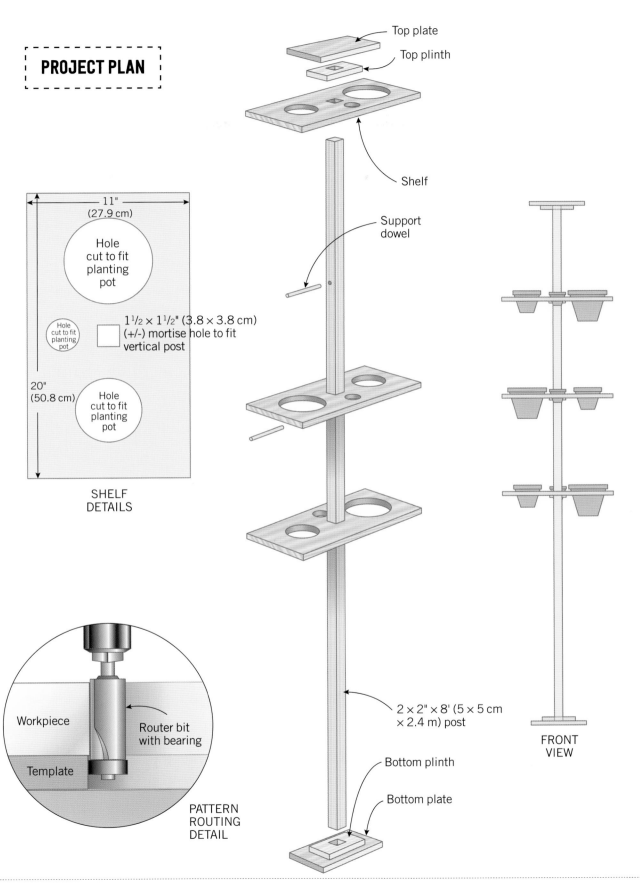

Top plate

Top plinth

Shelf

Support
dowel

11"
(27.9 cm)

Hole
cut to fit
planting
pot

Hole
cut to fit
planting
pot

$1^1/_2 \times 1^1/_2$" (3.8 × 3.8 cm)
(+/-) mortise hole to fit
vertical post

20"
(50.8 cm)

Hole
cut to fit
planting
pot

SHELF
DETAILS

2×2" × 8' (5 × 5 cm
× 2.4 m) post

Bottom plinth

Bottom plate

FRONT
VIEW

Workpiece

Router bit
with bearing

Template

PATTERN
ROUTING
DETAIL

PUTTING IT TOGETHER

Although this project is minimalist in appearance and material requirements, it isn't so minimal in the technique required to produce it. This project will require accurate chiseling work for it to be stable, as the shelves are held in place by their snug mortises (holes), through which the main vertical pieces pass. You will need to cut two mortises for the top and bottom blocks, and one through the center of each shelf.

1. Measure the vertical measurement the main support will have to span. Cut the 2 × 2" (5.1 × 5.1 cm) piece to that length.

2. Cut your shelves from your deck boards. The model seen here uses shelves that are 11 × 20" (27.9 × 50.8 cm).

3. Cut your top and bottom plinths from your deck boards. (A plinth is a base to support a column. In this project, two plinths have been stacked on the bottom and there are two at the top.) The small plinths measure 7 × 4" (17.8 × 10.2 cm) and the large plinths are 12 × 5.5" (30.5 × 14 cm).

4. Using the off-cut from the 2 × 2" (5.1 × 5.1 cm), use your sharp pencil or marking knife to trace the shape of the 2 × 2" (5.1 × 5.1 cm) onto the center of one of your end blocks. Staying well within the lines, drill out the majority of the material with your drill.

5. Very carefully, begin chiseling away material to form the clean mortise through the shelf. A $^3/_4$" (1.9 cm), sharp wood chisel should do the job. You want to sneak up on your line and make your final chisel cut take off only a small amount. A chisel will drive away from vertical if you attempt to take too large a cut. There are many good videos on YouTube showing good chiseling and mortising technique. The proper sharpness of your chisel will go a long way to making this a fun task.

Note: An alternative and much faster approach would be to use a technique called template routing using a router, brass bushing, and a template. If you had a $^3/_4$" (1.9 cm) bushing, and $^1/_2$" (1.3 cm) spiral bit, you would create a template that has $^1/_{16}$" (0.2 cm) larger hole than your 2 × 2" (5.1 × 5.1 cm). Then, you could clamp this to your workpiece and template route. There are also videos on template routing if this more advanced technique is interesting to you. It has more setup required but produces a perfect mortise every time in a fraction of the time. A situation such as this, where you want to cut, potentially, six or more identical mortises, is a perfect application for template routing. Be aware that template routing is a relatively advanced woodworking technique. If you choose to try it, practice on some wood scraps first until you get the hang of it.

6. Once you can squeeze your pole through the mortise, cut similar mortises for the rest of your shelves.

7. Cut two or three holes for the pots in each shelf using your jigsaw. A protractor can be very handy in this situation to draw the circles. Or, trace the actual pots.

8. Once you have your mortises cut, slide your shelves down the main vertical support. The mortises should be tight enough that they stay in place on their own.

9. Slip the plinths on the top and bottom with a bit of wood glue and set the assembly in its resting place.

10. Snug up the plinths to the ground/ceiling and screw them in place.

11. Using your $^3/_8$" (1 cm) drill bit, drill perfectly perpendicular holes through your vertical where you want the shelves to be.

12. Push a 3 to 4" (7.6 to 10.2 cm) dowel through the hole and slide the shelf down onto the dowel. That's all that's needed to support the shelves! The shear strength of wood across the grain is quite high, and as long as your mortises are tight, this is more than strong enough to hold the weight of the pots.

13. Apply a finish, if desired, and place your planted pots in their respective holes.

Dowels are used to hold the shelves in place. Shelves can be shimmied up and down the main pole until the desired levels are decided upon before adding the dowels.

The vertical structure works much like a shower curtain rod, though vertically, instead of horizontally. You simply have to adjust the top and bottom pieces to wedge it into place between the ground and porch roof. Modifications can be made to make this a standalone structure without a roof to hold it in place, but you would need to secure it to the ground.

CHAPTER 3
FRONT YARD FLOWERS, FOLIAGE, AND GROUNDCOVER

When I started gardening at the rental homes I lived in as a young adult and later on the property of my first home, the purpose of plants in my front yard garden was purely aesthetic. Any perennial I chose was a design choice to fill a specific hole in the landscape, and annuals were purchased to fit with a different color scheme each year.

But as my enthusiasm for gardening grew, so, too, did a new awareness. I was reading a lot of new gardening books and was drawn to magazines and newspaper articles on a vast range of topics related to gardening—from attracting beneficial insects to the garden and feeding pollinators to gardening with less water and dealing with excessive water. Working at and writing for gardening publications further helped guide me toward a more mindful approach to gardening. Over the years, I've also learned from other gardeners (including my two Savvy Gardening business partners), talks, and documentaries. Whether deliberately or not, I've been consistently exposed to new research and ideas. And it's so nice to see a new generation of gardeners starting their learning from this point of environmental awareness.

My approach hasn't become more complicated, but I like the word "mindful" to describe how I now choose many plants. Don't get me wrong, I still choose plants based on looks—foliage, stunning blooms, texture, and more. But many of my choices are now based on various characteristics of the plants, such as drought tolerance and pest resistance.

Getting back to the front yard itself, there are many possibilities, as our focus on the lawn diminishes in importance. On my own property, I grow salt-tolerant plants along the curb because my front garden gets its fair share of salt spray from winter plows. Many of these plants are also drought-tolerant bloomers that don't mind the hot, dry days of summer without a deep drink (not to mention poor soil, which I'm consistently working to amend).

And my ambition is, eventually, to transform great swaths of lawn into more garden. I know such an endeavour takes planning and time—and plants. And certainly as perennials fill in, keeping the weeds down would be a big perpetual item on my to-do list. But the long-term goal is a low-maintenance haven that welcomes wildlife and insects.

Driving through neighborhoods everywhere reveals more of a balance between perfect grass and gardens—especially on smaller lots, where the effort doesn't seem quite so overwhelming.

Credit: (opposite) Tara Nolan

TO HAVE GRASS OR NOT TO HAVE GRASS . . .

There is no right or wrong answer! I do think the days of every homeowner having a picture-perfect emerald-green lawn with nary a weed or hint of clover are waning. A walk through a neighborhood will likely reveal more of a mix of grassless front yard gardens than, say, twenty years ago. What's frustrating about some homes with traditional lawns is the relentless watering they require during a heat wave. It's such a senseless waste of a valuable resource. And then there are the lawns that have been sprayed with cosmetic pesticides and/or herbicides, making them essentially barren wastelands to pollinators.

I allow the parts of my property that are still lawn to go dormant in the summer. In that state it can look quite dead, especially on the hill by my driveway, but I have to relinquish that ingrained notion that a lawn has to look lush and green, even during extreme heat. These days, my sprinkler only comes out if someone wants to cool off on a hot summer day.

Lawns do have their place. Often when driving by homes with big properties, I ruminate over how hard it would be to convert such a big space to a garden. Although mowing and edging and weed whacking take time and effort, so, too, do gardens. But grass does have its benefits: It works to control soil erosion, traps pollution, and absorbs and sequesters carbon. It even helps reduce noise pollution. A grass lawn is also mandatory with many homeowners associations (HOAs)—though I would hope they don't focus so much on keeping them green during extreme heat.

I got rid of all the grass on the lawn of my previous home because of a recurring grub problem—and the fun design challenge of converting grass to garden. My current home has a very well-established lawn that the home's previous owner took great pride in, but eventually I'd like to transform more of it into garden, too (it's a project my husband and I will chip away at over time). For the grass that remains, we've started to overseed in the spring with more low-maintenance varieties. There is a magic to walking through the cool grass in your bare feet during a hot summer day.

I enjoy more of a wild look, and it would be great to see this softer, more untamed appearance, even in yards where the homeowner wants to keep grass. I also love how there are some naturalized bulbs mixed in here. Credit: Tara Nolan

ECO-FRIENDLIER GRASS OPTIONS TO INVESTIGATE

If you want that traditional carpet of turfgrass in your front yard, look for lower-maintenance, drought-tolerant varieties that will do well in all conditions—from full sun to shade. Much research is going into figuring out how those who still want lawns—or organizations who rely on lawns (golf courses, schools, and so on)—can choose varieties that are more sustainable and less taxing on the environment.

Look for blends formulated for your region (cool season versus warm season) that are heat and drought tolerant, if possible.

Eco-Lawn, a grass seed blend from a company called Wildflower Farm (see Resources, page 199) is a mix featuring several fescue varieties that result in a slow-growing, drought-tolerant lawn. Fescues don't require as much mowing. I like the soft, wilder look of fescue grasses and feel tempted to maintain a smaller lawn with these varieties.

Homeowners who want a low-maintenance, more drought-tolerant lawn can plant seed varieties such as those included in Eco-Lawn. Credit: wildflowerfarm.com

Clovers and micro clovers are other options that have been researched and tested by turf experts looking for eco-friendly alternatives to traditional grass. Micro clover has smaller leaves than the more traditional Dutch white clover, but still manages to crowd out weeds while adding nitrogen to grass when interplanted with low-maintenance grass varieties—and it's soft under the feet, less of a target for grubs, and is drought resistant. And, it's green. When overseeding, try mixing a bit in with fescue varieties.

Check with local seed companies to find low-maintenance lawn options that don't require as much maintenance as traditional grass seed.

ADD A CUT FLOWER GARDEN TO YOUR FRONT YARD

Even if you don't have a specific cutting garden, you can mix some vase-worthy beauties, like dahlias, into your planting scheme.
Credit: Nick McCullough

O ne of my favorite crops to grow is flowers. I call them "crops" because my intention when I plant certain varieties is to harvest the blooms. I love snipping fresh flowers and foliage for summer arrangements. I grow annual flowers, such as cosmos and zinnias, for my vases, and I "shop" my yard for foliage, like hosta leaves and ninebark branches. In spring, my first "cut flowers" are from the forsythia branches I bring indoors to force and brighten up my home.

Of course if you plan ahead, you can plant extra flowers so you have some that are destined for bouquets whereas others can remain in the garden for you and your neighbors to enjoy. This is always my dilemma with peonies. I love peony bouquets in May and June when they bloom, but I'm judicious with my snipping so I can enjoy the plant outdoors, too.

Full sun is the best scenario for a front yard cutting garden. As with any garden you start, Sarah Nixon (see Meet an Urban Flower Farmer, page 60) affirms that a successful cut flower garden begins with soil health. Build healthy nutrient-rich soil with lots of microbial activity—and remove your perennial weeds. That's an important step.

If you have a blank canvas, great! If not, intermingle your annual flowers with existing perennials, such as peonies. Other perennials that make great cut flowers include black-eyed Susans, echinacea, coreopsis, lavender, disease-resistant roses that are hardy to your climate, and hydrangeas.

Sarah recommends planting your cut flower choices in blocks. She'll also work with what's existing in a garden, so if you have established perennials, you could incorporate them. For Sarah, when plants are grouped in blocks, not only is it easy for her to find her plants when they're all together, but different flowers have different needs—nutrients, sun, and watering requirements.

Karen Bertelsen of The Art of Doing Stuff grows a selection of cut flowers in her raised beds for summer bouquets.
Credit: Karen Bertelsen

EASY CUT FLOWERS TO GROW INCLUDE:

Cosmos
Dahlia
Disease-resistant roses hardy to your climate
Nasturtium
Sunflower
Zinnia

ADD SOME SHRUBS TO THE MIX SO YOU CAN ADD FOLIAGE (AND MAYBE THE ADDED BONUS OF FLOWERS) TO YOUR BOUQUETS WITH:

Clematis
Cotoneaster
Forsythia
Japanese privet
Lilac
Ninebark
Scented geranium
Weigela

In this corner lot, the side and backyard are both open to the street. Sarah has planted shiso, dahlia 'Wine-Eyed Jill', cosmos, carnation 'Chabaud Jeanne Dionis', and zinnia 'Benary's Giant Wine'.
Credit: Sarah Nixon

In this front yard, Sarah is growing dahlias, rose mallow (both the pink and white flowers), and Rudbeckia 'Sahara'. Credit: Sarah Nixon

MEET AN URBAN FLOWER FARMER

My Luscious Backyard is an urban flower farm and floral design company. Owner, Sarah Nixon, practices micro-farming in her city using residential front yards and backyards (mostly front yards) to grow high-intensity, cut flower gardens. She harvests flowers for floral design work—weekly subscriptions and weddings. She also sells seedlings and dahlia tubers, and sells flowers wholesale to some florists.

Sarah became consumed by growing flowers in her urban backyard. "I wanted to grow flowers and started to bring them into the house to be with them up close," she recalls. She started selling some of her blooms at a local farmers' market, but was running out of space to grow them.

Before she launched her business in 2002, Sarah didn't realize small-scale flower farming was a thing. She says a book called *The Flower Farmer* by Lynn Byczynski gave her the confidence to imagine she could actually make a living growing flowers on a small scale. She decided to approach acquaintances who lived nearby to ask whether she could use their extraneous space. "They were really open to someone beautifying their space and using it and then benefitting from not having to mow their lawn anymore," she says. Sarah now manages several properties in her neighborhood. "Growing flowers was a way for me to feel connected to the natural world that was so important to me growing up in rural Vancouver Island."

A DAYLILY ENTHUSIAST USES HIS FRONT YARD TO BREED NEW VARIETIES

Paul Gellatly, curatorial gardener at the Toronto Zoo, is renting his home and only has access to the front yard. Before converting grass to garden, he asked permission of his landlord because, when he eventually moves out, he'll take most of the plants with him. The landlord was happy with Paul's plans.

In his 35 × 40' (10.7 × 12.2 m) garden, Paul breeds daylilies (at the time of writing, there are about 400). He has nine registrations with the American Hemerocallis Society with six or more in the works.

Besides his daylily collection, this self-confessed zone pusher has planted thirty Japanese maples, two magnolia trees, three ginkgo (maidenhair) trees, a monkey puzzle tree, a *Paulownia tomentosa* (Empress tree) that had reached 25' (7.6 m) tall after being planted from seed five years prior, and "a bunch of rare and unusual perennials."

Sadly, when he eventually moves out, Paul says he'll grass over the garden, but maybe the landlord or the next tenants will feel compelled to fill in the holes with new plants and continue to garden.

Paul's plants in his front yard garden are meticulously tagged.
Credit: Paul Gellatly

Paul sells his daylilies from his driveway. He has more than 200 cultivars and hundreds of seedlings in the garden. This one is named after popular Canadian singer Jann Arden. Credit: Paul Gellatly

POLLINATOR MAGNETS

Research pollinator-friendly plants to fill any holes you may have in the garden. Credit: Nick McCullough

Gardeners everywhere, by this time, should be well aware of the importance of integrating a plan to support pollinators in the garden. There are wonderful resources available underlining the magnitude of insect population decline and rich with ideas about what homeowners can do to help. As habitat becomes scarcer, we green thumbs have the opportunity to roll out a welcome mat of pollinator-friendly plants in our yards, no matter what size they are—in-ground gardens, window boxes, hanging fabric pockets for flowers, containers—they all count.

Bees, as well as the monarch butterfly, are the most common pollinators that show up in headlines, but there are thousands of species of native bees, butterflies, moths, hummingbirds, wasps, flies, beetles, and more that we can support in our gardens.

Don't just think about food for the pollinators; think about providing sources of habitat and water. Here are some plants that will attract pollinators to your garden.

PLANTS TO ATTRACT POLLINATORS

PERENNIALS	ANNUALS
Aster	Borage
Black-eyed Susan	Calendula
Butterfly weed	Celosia (great
Buttonbush	for living and
Chives	dried cut-flower
Coreopsis	arrangements)
Echinacea	Cornflower, or
Liatris	bachelor's buttons
Ninebark	Cosmos
Potentilla	Marigold
Rose of Sharon	Nasturtium
Sedum, zone	Sunflower
depends on variety	
Shasta daisy	

An urban front yard garden featuring
pollinator-friendly plants.
Credit: Jim Charlier

MEADOWS AND WILDFLOWERS

I became attuned to a naturalistic planting style when I first viewed the densely planted expanse filled with beautiful swaths of perennials in a variety of textures and colors that greets visitors at the Toronto Botanical Garden. It was the work of Dutch garden designer Piet Oudolf. Those swaths, more accurately described as drifts of grasses and perennials, are a key design component of the New Perennial movement, where the life cycle of the entire plant, from bud to bloom to seed head are taken into consideration to provide year-round structure and visual interest in the garden.

Another key element to the success of this garden is fluidity of design—groupings of plants, rather than blocks, are intermingled in seemingly random drifts that make it look less intentional, even though it very much is.

The types of plants are also very specifically chosen for their structural properties. Tony Spencer on his website *The New Perennialist*, explains: "For purposes of design, Oudolf encourages us to think of the herbaceous kingdom as a series of spires, globes, daisies, buttons, spikes, plumes, and umbels, as well as the textural effects that various plants can create. The plants you choose with these characteristics can be categorized into layers—structural (trees and shrubs, grasses, and taller perennials), companion plants, groundcover, vertical plants, and filler plants (these can be annuals and bulbs)."

Oudolf's design style, when applied to the scale of an urban front yard, can be quite stunning. There is a mindfulness and deliberateness to the drifts—the key is to intermingle the layers to get that natural, unplanned look. This concept ties in nicely to a central theme in this book, which is the idea of working with nature instead of against it: that is, knowing your growing conditions and planting accordingly. Furthermore, it pushes back against the notion of paving over paradise. Naturalistic planting is about embracing nature.

Wildscaping is a term more recently conceived by Tony Spencer. He is a part of the New Perennial Movement of plant designers, and is experimenting with his interpretation and progression of what naturalistic planting is and means to a gardener.

"Wildscaping is about using plant-driven landscape design, inspired by the wildness of nature, to create gardens with a sense of both beauty and purpose to rekindle our relationship to the natural world," he explains.

In a front yard, Tony says the question is: How can you create a plant community that's designed to flow together? It's a matter of looking to nature for both aesthetic and ecological inspiration to be able to understand how to do things.

Layering is also a very important part of the planning and then the planting process as well as deciding on the balance of plants, like the ratio of perennials to ornamental grasses. If you look at natural models, such as a forest, you'll see that the layered structure starts with the canopy, followed by the sub canopy, the understory layers of trees, and so on.

The Entry Garden Walk at the Toronto Botanical Garden, designed by garden designer Piet Oudolf. Credit: Janet Davis

Plant layering at the Piet Oudolf-designed Lurie Garden in Chicago. Credit: Niki Jabbour

Then, you can apply that idea of layers to what you'll plant in the garden. The major grasses and perennials, as well as trees and shrubs, form that structural layer that anchors the design. The seasonal theme layer can be perennials with various bloom times, as well as annuals (or bulbs for that spring interest). Groundcover is important, and, as Tony points out, it's a functional layer in German design because it suppresses weeds and acts as a living mulch.

"Scatter plants" refer to certain repeated plants that appear through the entire planting and help give it a feeling of cohesion and unity. What pulled this whole concept of wildscaping together for me was the idea of considering your plants, not as a collection, but rather as a community. Just as a natural woodland would have various species living in harmony (let's pretend invasive species don't exist), you choose plants that coexist well and group them by common habitat, in whatever conditions your property offers in terms of sunlight, moisture, and soil.

Circling back to groundcover, Tony speaks to how easy it is for the garden design to fall into place when you plant with a matrix-style approach. The matrix is the groundcover layer that you can start with, followed by adding the structural bits and experimenting with fitting other plants into the puzzle.

Having a mix of native plants and non-native plants is okay, as it opens up your palette and your options. And, it offers greater amplitude in terms of biodiversity. The most important thing is the relationship the plants have with each other.

With wildscaping, Tony says beauty in a garden is no longer only what's in bloom and what looks pretty; it's also seeing the path the plant takes throughout the entire year—from bud to bloom to seed head to skeleton. The concept of beauty can be more open. There is senescence and depth. "It's a philosophical thing as much as anything else."

Above: When creating his pond garden, Tony consulted with Piet Oudolf, who recommended that he not plant a crowd of plants that all come up at the same time, but, rather, he encouraged him to have some quieter and lower elements in the planting. Right: Tony has applied a matrix-style approach to the plantings on his own property.
Credit: Tony Spencer

- Trying for a natural flow—think asymmetrically and organically

- Keeping things low input, high output

- Dealing with the conditions you have

- In terms of the maintenance, during that first year of establishment, planting things close enough together to allow plants to lock, or grow into each other, over time (hopefully, this keeps the weeding down)

- Being prepared to get out there with your Dutch hoe that first year or so to keep after the weeds

- Leaving the plants stand throughout the winter, not only for aesthetic reasons, but also for the benefit of the insects

- In spring (once temperatures are consistently above 50°F [10°C], using a trimmer or mulch mower and letting the detritus sit and replenish the soil for the following year

- Letting bulbs and later the perennials push up through the debris

Tony Spencer describes this efficiently planted urban garden that takes advantage of a small space as "the urbane front garden of Barry Parker." Even in this small space, the color and texture of the Hakonechloa 'Albo-Striata', allium 'Purple Sensation', and hosta work together to create a lush, vibrant groundcover. Credit: Tony Spencer

Plant a little Irish moss between stepping stones and it will start to spread over thyme—I mean time. Credit: Donna Griffith

Delosperma 'Fire Spinner' is a striking heat- and drought-tolerant groundcover with gorgeous orange and fuchsia flowers. Credit: Tara Nolan

THE MAGIC OF GROUNDCOVER

Underneath perennials, or in the absence of grass, sometimes it's nice to fill in a space with a low-growing groundcover. My first introduction to the impact of groundcover in a garden was in my mom's front yard garden growing up. 'Dragon's Blood' stonecrop spread with controlled abandon underneath a pea shrub and around the perennials below. It cascaded over a decorative rock and the bees absolutely loved it! The spreader also provided year-round interest. In my current home, I have a chartreuse variety of sedum with yellow flowers that was in my gardens when I moved in. It likes to pop up unannounced throughout my gardens, but I don't mind. It is extremely drought tolerant and adds welcome hits of color.

Groundcovers are a great way to fill in a space around a tree to add another layer in front of a grouping of plants of various heights. They can also be used as a solution to fill in gaps between pathways. Depending on which varieties you choose, they can look nice through all the seasons. Another bonus? They cover the space that weeds might otherwise occupy (though do keep an eye out for the more pernicious ones that like to sneak in when you aren't looking). And going back to the grass discussion, groundcover can also take the place of grass.

For areas that get a bit of traffic—perhaps you have a few stepping stones peppered throughout your front yard garden—look for walkable or treadable groundcovers, such as Irish moss or woolly thyme. It's worth noting that some walkable groundcover plants may be labeled "treadable," but they are sensitive to constant foot traffic. Check the plant tag to confirm.

Groundcover can also be used to great effect on a natural driveway. Of course, if your car leaks any type of fluid it won't be good for the plants but, otherwise, a strip of mixed groundcover between the areas where the two tires sit can look quite stunning. See page 175 for my Sedum Driveway Project.

One thing to note is that some groundcovers can be quite invasive and/or aggressive. On my current property, I have one nice semicircle area of goutweed (planted by the previous owner). I actually quite like the variegated foliage and have managed to keep it in check. On the other hand, a patch of ajuga, which is often recommended as a walkable groundcover, seems to be trying to spread through my lawn. It's pretty when in bloom, but it needs serious taming. So do be careful with what you choose.

PLANTING A GROUNDCOVER QUILT

For one of his clients, landscape designer Sean James planted, what he refers to as, a "groundcover quilt" in the front yard.

Sean says that, often, when gardeners choose groundcover, they choose one to fill in an area, but cautions you could be setting yourself up for failure. If a problem arises, it wipes out everything. Introducing biodiversity adds resilience to the planting scheme—and you benefit from having something in bloom at different times of the year.

When it came to placing plants, Sean tried to avoid, what he refers to as, jumble syndrome. "If you mix things up too much people don't see beauty in it," he explains. So plants were placed in mass groups of five and seven. Attention was paid to form and texture. As everything fills in, it will knit together, performing as the different "patches" of the quilt.

Sean focused a lot on evergreen groundcover. This means during winters, where snow isn't as prevalent, there's still something to look at when the garden is uncovered. One other element is a dry bed (sometimes called an arroyo) that cuts through the middle of the front yard, diverting rainwater from a downspout away from the house.

One bonus of the groundcover quilt? It eliminates mowing. Once established, it's lower maintenance than a lawn. Furthermore, you increase your rainwater infiltration while adding interest to your property. Sean does add one proviso: That first year you have to be emotionally prepared to water and weed to get over the "establishment hump." As the groundcover spreads and the plants fill in, the workload will ebb. In the meantime, don't install more than you can look after.

Landscape designer Sean James has planted, what he refers to as, a "groundcover quilt" for a client. As it grows in, it will create a colorful tapestry in a front yard in place of turfgrass. Plants include bergenia, *Carex pensylvanica*, *Veronica peduncularis* 'Georgia Blue', armeria, 'Tidal Pool' hybrid Veronica, *Phlox stolonifera*, white rock cress (Arabis), a couple of the *Juniperus horizontalis* varieties, black mondo grass, 'Golden Tiara' hosta, and Opuntia.
Credit: Donna Griffith

As it grows in, this groundcover quilt will create a colorful tapestry in the front yard in place of turfgrass. Credit: Donna Griffith

Armeria maritima
Credit: Donna Griffith

PLANT FOR FOUR-SEASON INTEREST

A four-season garden is one that will provide little sections of interest from spring through winter. If you're going the perennial route, choose a mix of varieties so there is always something in bloom in the front yard garden. And be mindful of the power of foliage as leaves can change color throughout each season. I have a euphorbia, for example, with foliage that emerges as green/red in spring, followed by a topping of vibrant yellow flowers, and then settling in to a gorgeous green/red, and then a deep crimson in fall. Although it may require a bit of planning, laying out a four-season garden doesn't have to be a daunting task.

In garden writer Ken Brown's front garden, an assortment of vibrant spring bulbs fade away to reveal established perennials. Credit: Ken Brown

If you have some time in your planning process, visit the nursery or garden center in each season to see what is available and take a walk around your neighborhood to see how various plants are incorporated into the landscape. You might notice all the blossoms of a purple sand cherry in spring and the echinacea abuzz with pollinators in summer. Taking brisk fall walks is how I discovered and fell in love with Japanese anemones. A few years ago, I saw these gorgeous pink flowers with yellow centers in a fall garden. I didn't know what they were until 'Honorine Jobert' was named the 2016 Perennial Plant of the Year.

Pay careful attention to plant tags to ensure you're placing the plant in optimal growing conditions.

"I finally gave up trying to have perfect sod in the south," says landscape designer Nancy Wallace of Wallace Gardens. **"We had many years of drought and it required an enormous amount of water to keep it green. In addition, I live on a heavily shaded lot and, as the trees got bigger, they cast more and more shade, making it nearly impossible to keep enough light on the sod to make it look good. I prepared a landscape plan eliminating all the front sod, submitted it to my HOA, and, surprisingly, they allowed me to proceed. No more front lawn!"**
Credit: Nancy Wallace

Garden writer and photographer Janet Davis has strategically planted her front garden, so that something shines in every season: tulips, poet's narcissus, and camassia in spring; echinacea, Russian sage, black-eyed Susans, and liatris in summer; and New England asters, fothergillas, and sedum 'Autumn Joy' in autumn. Sedums, rudbeckias, and fothergilla are left standing to provide winter interest.
Credit: Janet Davis

PLANTING UNDER A BLACK WALNUT TREE

Black walnuts are an interesting variety of tree. Not only do they repel many plants by producing a chemical called juglone, but the walnuts are like little projectile baseballs when they eventually plummet off the tree. Though these trees are prized for their hardwood, for homeowners, they can become the bane of their green-thumbed existence (not unlike various nefarious weeds).

And if one small urban front yard happens to be the home of a black walnut tree, it can be a challenge to plant anything under it.

So, what, exactly, can be planted under or around a black walnut tree? Surprisingly, quite a few plants will fare well, whereas others, when planted within 50 to 60' (15.2 to 18.3 m) of the root zone, will, essentially, wither and die.

Trees and shrubs tolerant of juglone include spring favorites elderberry, redbud, and forsythia, as well as rose of Sharon and ninebark. Tolerant plants include hosta, purple coneflower, sweet woodruff, Siberian iris, black-eyed Susan, and summer phlox. Even spring bulbs, such as tulips, grape hyacinth, and daffodils, can be planted underneath the black walnut tree.

TOO SALTY: DEALING WITH SALINATED SOIL

Credit: Shutterstock

In winter, I try to use eco-friendly, de-icers for my driveway and pathways and only when absolutely necessary. But I can't help what gets plowed or sprayed onto my front garden, which extends right to the curb, from the road. My municipality uses road salt. I live on a hill, so during an especially slippery winter, it gets doused pretty often.

Not only is road salt harmful to plants and turfgrass, the salt also eats at pavement and concrete, not to mention its inevitable runoff into storm drains. This leads to the contamination of groundwater, lakes, and rivers, which can harm wildlife and freshwater organisms.

According to the Soil Science Society of America, "Once deposited, components of salts, particularly sodium ions, can wreak havoc on soil systems. They do this by reducing the soil's ability to retain plant nutrients and water, and maintain soil structure." And, it can take a long time for salt buildup to wash away.

If you have plants in a garden close to a roadway or perhaps a municipally cleared sidewalk that is regularly salted, you might want to ensure your front line of plants is salt tolerant. One thing to note is that synthetic and organic fertilizers also add salt to soil. If you're concerned about what's in your soil, consider having it tested.

Annuals don't do well in oversalinated soil, and some perennials, such as Japanese maples, are very sensitive to it as well. There are certain signs that can help you determine if your plants are affected by road salt buildup: they become stunted and stop growing new leaves; they develop a blue-green tinge to the leaves or smaller leaves turn yellow and wilt; and the plant's leaves look like they have been burned.

Columbine
Credit: Tara Nolan

Asclepias tuberosa
Credit: Tara Nolan

Daylily
Credit: Tara Nolan

Gaillardia
Credit: Tara Nolan

Here is a list of plants to consider that will tolerate varying degrees of salt. Your local garden center may have a solid list of options as well.

PLANTS WITH MODERATE SALT TOLERANCE

Asclepias tuberosa (butterfly weed)
Bellflower *Campanula*
Catmint *Nepeta*
Creeping thyme
Russian sage *Perovskia atriplicifolia*
Sedum 'Autumn Joy' (Autumn stonecrop)
Silver mound Artemisia *Artemisia schmidtiana* ('Silver Mound')
Yarrow *Achillea*

PLANTS WITH HIGH SALT TOLERANCE

Blanket flower *Gaillardia*
Blue Lyme Grass *Leymus arenarius*
Chinese Fountain Grass *Pennisetum alopecuroides*
Columbine *Aquilegia*
Daylilies
Dianthus
'Elijah Blue' fescue *Festuca glauca* 'Elijah Blue'
'Karl Foerster' reed grass *Calmagrostis acutifolia* 'Karl Foerster'
Lady's mantle *Alchemilla mollis*
Sea thrift *Armeria*

CONTAINER GARDENING IDEAS

Even if you only have a small front yard space, a well-planted container—or a grouping of containers—can deliver a big impact. For those who want more of a grab-and-go-option, clever growers and nursery owners have started creating mixes planted together from the get-go and that are delivered fully grown and often in bloom in the pot. It takes much of the guesswork out of container gardening and can make it very easy for a busy homeowner to add some life and color to their doorstep with minimal effort.

If you enjoy putting together your own containers, it can be really enjoyable to get those creative juices flowing to piece them together each season, figuring out a palette, sussing out new plants, and looking for height, texture, and "spiller" qualities.

Sunblaze miniature roses bloom from spring through fall and are perfect choices for ornamental pots. Credit: Star Roses & Plants

Switching it up each season is also fun. In springtime, start with cold-tolerant plants, like bulbs (tulips, hyacinth, daffodils), pansies with their sweet little faces, and flowering branches, like forsythia, pussy willow, etc. For summer, think show-stopping blooms, such as dahlia, petunia, *Calibrachoa*, etc. Add texture with foliage from coleus to coral bells to herbs. For fall, think harvest colors and plants that won't mind a touch of frost, such as mums and asters and ornamental cabbage. Winter gives you a bit of a break because you don't really have to worry about watering or deadheading when you put together an arrangement of evergreen boughs.

THE POWER OF POTSCAPING

Potscaping is a word that has gained popularity as green thumbs who live in small spaces have gotten creative with their gardening. You don't need a physical plot to have a garden. You can plant in pots, sub-irrigated planters, fabric containers, paint buckets, old washbasins— anything, really. And once you arrange them, well, that's potscaping!

Balcony gardeners are familiar with the obvious necessity of using pots to create a garden. But I first saw the term *potscaping* used in an editorial spread when I worked as the web editor at *Canadian Gardening* magazine. The term doesn't really describe landscaping with pots, per se, it's more of the artistic arrangement of the pots themselves. In some cases, it's almost as if you are creating a garden out of pots. In others, it might be more of a vertical shelving arrangement of pots. I've also seen pots carefully placed here and there among actual planted gardens. When placed well, they can look really artistic and blend in to a front yard garden design. Whether you have three pots to display or thirty, the key is in the arranging.

This home uses the power of potscaping to create a lush garden around a garage—there must be a separate entrance! Credit: Roger Yip

Opuntia and succulents steal the show in this front stoop display. Credit: Roger Yip

This compact rose, called Rainbow Knock Out Rose, is hardy down to -30°F (-34°C), with peachy-pink flowers. It will thrive in a container, if planted correctly. Credit: Star Roses & Plants

PLANTING PERENNIALS IN POTS

Containers needn't be reserved just for growing veggies or to create a standout arrangement. Sometimes, one simple perennial planted in a pot will add visual impact. And with an every-increasing selection of compact plants to choose from, they are a great way to enjoy the benefits of a garden if you don't have the space. Carefully consult the plant tag and maybe even the grower's website to get as much planting info as possible when choosing a plant for a pot. Make sure you can provide adequate drainage and planting depth and diameter for your plant, as well as ongoing maintenance, including pruning and fertilizing.

CHOOSING THRILLERS, FILLERS, AND SPILLERS

Creeping rosemary is used here as a spiller. Add an assortment of herbs to your pots. It's a great way to sneak more food into your gardens! Credit: Donna Griffith

Here, alyssum acts as a filler, whereas a showy *Calibrachoa*—Superbells Double Blue Calibrachoa from Proven Winners—with its rosebud-like double blooms could be considered both a thriller *and* a spiller. Credit: Donna Griffith

I'm not sure who came up with the whole thrillers, fillers, and spillers catchphrase, but it's a succinct, apt explanation when describing how to plant a container. Nurseries often organize their stock to easily help consumers choose plants. Personally, I like to push the envelope a little and include something more unexpected.

In short, a "thriller" is that WOW plant—the stunner that will sit front and center. It commands all the attention. Examples of a good "thriller" are a showy dahlia or canna lily. You could also include a really stunning variety of petunia, supertunia, or *Calibrachoa*.

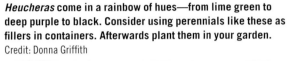

Heucheras come in a rainbow of hues—from lime green to deep purple to black. Consider using perennials like these as fillers in containers. Afterwards plant them in your garden. Credit: Donna Griffith

Left: In a shade garden, hostas can be the perfect thriller *and* filler. Above: Hostas can brighten up a dark, shady part of the garden. Look for miniature varieties for pots. Credit: Tara Nolan

"Fillers" are more compact plants that will fill in those holes to make the container look lush and full, such as alyssum, *Hypoestes*, coleus, begonia, etc. I like to use herbs as my fillers. I'll plant lemongrass, as an ornamental, in place of *Dracaena*.

Spillers are those plants that trail elegantly over the sides of the pot. These plants typically include sweet potato vine (there are some really lovely color and variegated options).

Plant lemongrass in place of that spike or *Dracaena* that you might include in a pot for its height. In full sun, it will grow to be quite high and full. Lemongrass can be dried for tea and is delicious in fall curries—so it's both edible and ornamental. Here, it's paired with Superbells Blackcurrant Punch Calibrachoa—a thriller for sure! Credit: Donna Griffith

For a while, petunias fell off my radar (and out of favor) because they can get leggy and need to be deadheaded. However, varieties like 'Night Sky', a pretty spectacular thriller, have changed my mind. Credit: Donna Griffith

It's kind of a toss-up here, as there is no clear "filler" winner. A variety of succulents have been artfully arranged to create a stunning container arrangement. Credit: Roger Yip

Add perennials to bigger containers that you can leave in over all seasons, but underplant each year with different combinations of colorful annuals.
Credit: Donna Griffith

Talk about contrast! Sweet potato vine, which is often recommended as a filler at garden centers, is paired with a purple oxalis—also a stunning thriller in this instance!
Credit: Roger Yip

ACCESSORIZE THE FRONT OF YOUR HOUSE WITH WINDOW BOXES

If your window frames or sills allow, window boxes are a great way to add color and embellishment to the front of your home, especially if you don't have the space to display plants elsewhere in your front yard. They also work well on railings.

Unless you want to get fancy with your joinery, building a wooden window box is a really easy endeavor for a novice woodworker. What's great about the project is you can customize the size. However, there are also some really great self-watering window boxes on the market, which are no-brainers if they fit aesthetically and physically into the intended location.

You can also find lightweight hanging fabric planters (if you are concerned about weight), where you can grow everything from ornamental flowers to lettuces.

If your window box destination is in a hot, sunny area, consider a collection of succulents for your arrangement. Credit: Roger Yip

It's amazing how quickly a window box can brighten a windowsill. It's a great project if you have scrap wood lying around.
Credit: Donna Griffith

Window boxes can add a lush vertical garden to your space—even if you don't have the square footage to garden in the ground!
Credit: Shutterstock.

TRASH AND RECYCLING BIN COVER WITH ROOFTOP GARDEN

DESIGNED AND BUILT BY JAMIE GILGEN OF CADENCE FURNITURE
PHOTOS BY DONNA GRIFFITH
ILLUSTRATION BY LEN CHURCHILL

N ot everyone has a garage or shed where they can keep their trash, compost, and recycling bins out of reach of neighborhood racoons or other pests. A trash bin cover is essentially a mini shed that will protect bins and keep them out of sight. But why not add a garden to it?

Inspired by rooftop gardens, I figured a trash bin cover was as good a spot as any to add a little bloom power. Depending on where it's situated, you could also sneak in veggies, like lettuces or herbs.

Whoever builds this beauty won't mind if it's visible from the street. There are a couple of modifications that can be made here and there, depending on the builder's tools and woodworking level of expertise. We've tried to note them as a bit of a "Choose Your Own Adventure" aspect to the project.

Note: The final dimensions for the cover are: 72" w × 49" h × 23" d (182.9 cm w × 124.5 cm h × 58.4 cm d)

TOOLS

Tape measure

Pencil

Miter saw, handsaw, or jig saw

Drill or impact driver

TOOLS FOR SHOU SUGI BAN (SEE PAGE 92)

Wire brush

Large torch

MATERIALS

One 6 × 6" × 12' (15.2 × 15.2 cm × 3.7 m) cedar post (for horizontal beams)

Two 4 × 4" × 8' (10.2 × 10.2 cm × 2.4 m) posts

Thirty 6 × 0.5 × 41" (15.24 × 1.3 × 104.1 cm) fence boards for cladding

Two 2 × 4" × 10' cedar (5.1 × 10.2 cm × 3 m) cedar for back and horizontals of door's Z frame

Three 2 × 4" × 10' cedar (5.1 × 10.2 cm × 3 m) cedar for sides and diagonals of door's Z frame

Two 6 × 0.5" × 8' (15.24 × 1.3 cm × 2.4 m) decking boards for short and long sides of raised bed box

Five 6 × 0.5" × 5' (15.24 × 1.3 × 1.5 m) fence boards for bottom of raised bed box

1¼" (3.2 cm) decking screws

3" (7.6 cm) decking screws

Hinges

4 L-brackets that are 3.5" (8.9 cm) wide (use if not doing mortise and tenon)

2 × 4" (5.1 × 10.2 cm) metal fence rail hangers (use if not doing mortise and tenon)

Drill drainage holes into the "roof" garden of your bin cover.

One of those modifications concerns the rooftop garden itself. Some may want to line the garden with an impermeable barrier and angle it so any water from rainfall or watering drains out and away from the back.

For this project, a removable tray was built for the garden/roof, drilled with holes for drainage, and lined with a semi-permeable landscape fabric. As builder Jamie Gilgen explained, her bins were already outside in the open anyhow, so a bit of water dripping through the roof garden into the "shed" wouldn't be a problem.

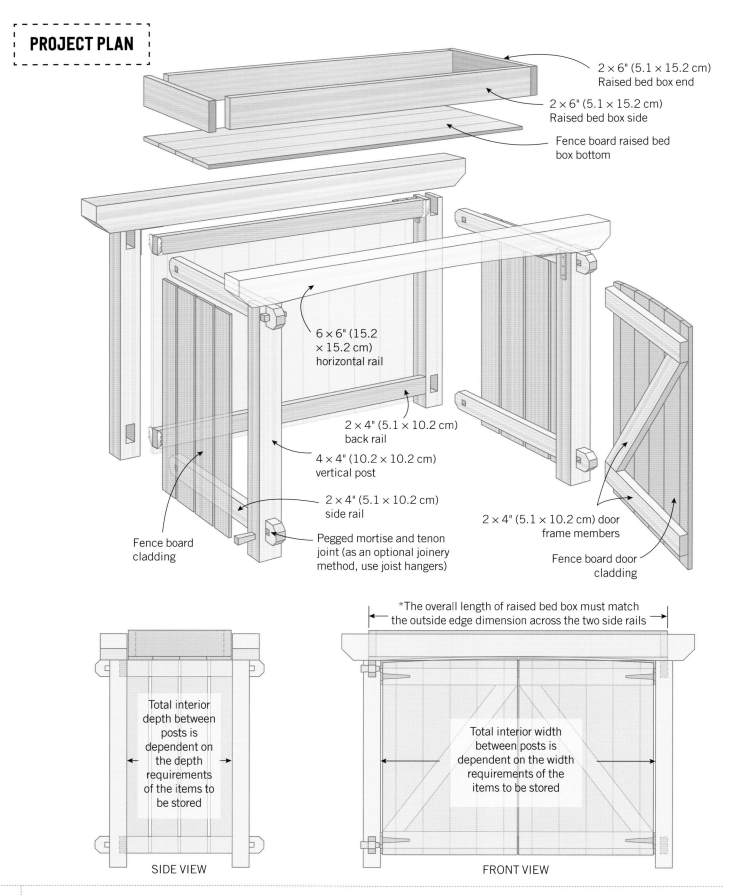

2 × 6" (5.1 × 15.2 cm)
Raised bed box end

2 × 6" (5.1 × 15.2 cm)
Raised bed box side

Fence board raised bed
box bottom

6 × 6" (15.2
× 15.2 cm)
horizontal rail

2 × 4" (5.1 × 10.2 cm)
back rail

4 × 4" (10.2 × 10.2 cm)
vertical post

2 × 4" (5.1 × 10.2 cm)
side rail

Fence board
cladding

Pegged mortise and tenon
joint (as an optional joinery
method, use joist hangers)

2 × 4" (5.1 × 10.2 cm) door
frame members

Fence board door
cladding

*The overall length of raised bed box must match
the outside edge dimension across the two side rails

Total interior
depth between
posts is
dependent on
the depth
requirements
of the items to
be stored

Total interior width
between posts is
dependent on the width
requirements of the
items to be stored

SIDE VIEW

FRONT VIEW

PUTTING IT TOGETHER

1. Cut your 6 × 6" × 12' (15.2 × 15.2 cm × 3.7 m) cedar post into two 6' (1.8 m)-long pieces. Measure the total width of your garbage can, green bin, and recycle boxes that will be straddled by the structure. Draw layout lines on the posts at the points where you'll attach your posts.

2. Cut your 4 × 4" (10.2 × 10.2 cm) posts to length (45" [114.5 cm] for mortise and tenon or 43" [109.2 cm] for bracket assembly) and then use either L-brackets or a mortise and tenon joint to attach the four vertical posts to the 6 × 6" × 6' (15.2 × 15.2 cm × 1.8 m) horizontal beam. If you want to put a profile (slight curve) into this beam, as shown in the photo, do this before you attach it to the vertical posts.

3. Once your 4 × 4" (10.2 cm × 10.2 cm) posts are attached, turn them right-side up and determine the depth of the cover required to fit your bins. If you're a more advanced woodworker, use a pegged mortise and tenon joint as shown in the photo example. For this project, the length was 35" (89 cm). If you're not using this method, measure four lengths of 2 × 4s and attach them with the metal fence rail hangers.

Builder's Note: For the mortise and tenon joinery, I used a router with a template bushing and a template, and then a flush-trim bit from the other side to take it all the way through. There are so many ways to cut mortises, but I chose this way because it's the simplest and most accurate and reproduce-able way to cut the joint.

4. Measure the distance between the two vertical posts attached to the rear cross beam and cut two more horizontal 2 × 4s to that length. They'll be 57" (144.8 cm) if you use a joist hanger, 61" (154.9 cm) if you use mortise and tenon. Attach them with metal fence rail hangers or mortise and tenon joinery. You now have the structure of your cover completed!

5. Determine the distance from the ground to the bottom of your beam and subtract 3" (7.6 cm) from this to find your fence board length. Cut some of your fence boards to this length (41" [104.1 cm]) and start attaching them to your cross member sides and back with 1¼" (3.1 cm) screws.

Do this all around your structure to close it in. You will need to experiment to get the best spacing between boards, depending on your measurements. Once you have a spacing you like, create a small spacer out of scrap wood and use this to set consistent gaps between each fence board.

6. For each door, cut two pieces for the top and bottom of the Z and one for the diagonal from a 2 × 4, making angled cuts so it forms the Z shape needed to fit the space. For the angle, line it up and draw the line on the diagonal that will make the Z frame work. Cut to that line. In the example build, the horizontals are 21" (53.3 cm) and the diagonal is 37⅛" (94.3 cm). Screw it together and attach the fence pickets.

7. Now, use your decking boards to create the raised bed box. Get measurements for your box from your structure and build the box. The box pictured is 21 × 62.25" (53.3 × 158.1 cm). It was made using four planks of wood, two of them 21" (53.3 cm) and two of them 62¼" (158 cm). The bottom planks are screwed on. Wood glue and screws were used here instead of fancy joinery.

You can use fence boards to make the bottom of the box. Make sure to use a type III wood glue, such as Titebond III, that will stand up to moisture. Drill drainage holes into the bottom of your box and place it on the structure. Fasten it down with 1¼" (3.2 cm) screws. Use landscape fabric to line the box and attach it with stainless steel staples. Fill it with soil and you're ready to plant.

Builder's Note: If you use the bracket assembly method, you may find that the structure racks. To prevent this, add diagonal members for rigidity inside the structure.

SHOU SUGI BAN

If you want, you can use a technique as shown in the model called *shou sugi ban*. This provides an aesthetically pleasing contrast in the wood and preserves it as well.

Start by using a very large torch to blacken the fence boards (before they have been attached). Once the wood has cooled, brush it down with a wire brush. That's it! You can repeat the process if you want a deeper black contrast. A natural oil is generally added to finish it. Interesting fact: This process of charring the wood actually makes it fire resistant.

A glimpse inside the trash bin cover. You may want to add a latch so the doors remain shut and cannot be opened by neighborhood pests, like raccoons.

A pegged mortise-and-tenon joint was used to secure the side rails. A small hammer was used to tap it in place.

This project features a removable "green roof" that sits perfectly on the top of the bin cover.

Before filling with soil, use stainless steel staples to attach landscape fabric into the inside of the "green roof."

CHAPTER 4
GROWING VEGETABLES IN FRONT YARDS

Years ago, when I lived in the big city, my route home from the bus stop took me past a tidy little bungalow with a tiny front garden. Instead of the typical foundation plantings—maybe a shrub or two and some annuals, there were always a couple of rows of tomato cages supporting multiple tomato plants. I marveled over this at the time because it was still fairly uncommon to see veggies in a front yard setting. But now, it's not uncommon to come across a raised bed or two, brimming with veggies in a front yard garden. You might even find an entire front yard devoted to growing fruits and vegetables.

Both urban and suburban properties can often present a challenge to green thumbs who are longing to grow edible plants. What to do if your backyard is in complete shadow? Perhaps there is a giant tree on the property, or in a neighbor's backyard, casting shade. (Or, possibly reaching its tentacled network of roots throughout the yard, making planting in the ground nearby next to impossible.) Raised beds can solve that problem, but if you don't have any light, it doesn't matter. The vegetables

need to be planted where the sunshine is. Sometimes the front yard happens to be a prime location for growing food because that's the area that gets the most sun.

Whatever the challenge, heat-loving veggies, such as tomatoes, melons, cucumbers, squash, peppers, and eggplants, need at least six to eight hours of sunlight a day to flourish. And, if it's your front yard that offers those optimal conditions, why not use the space in this way?

If you're not quite ready to commit to front yard rows of veggies planted in ground or in a raised bed, there are ways to scatter them throughout a landscape—cleverly tucked among the ornamental plants. Find a fancy obelisk and place it around a tomato that's been snuck in among perennials. Or, create a tidy row of edible edging along a garden border, using greens, like lettuce, spinach, kale, and herbs.

Kevin Espiritu, author of *Field Guide to Urban Gardening: How to Grow Plants, No Matter Where You Live*, lives in the "coveted zone 10b" in San Diego, California. His front yard garden is the only area where there is enough sun to grow food, so he says it's his de facto garden spot. Initially Kevin thought setting up a garden in a front yard urban setting might cause some issues, but he says it's been incredibly rewarding to see the reaction of his neighborhood and community. "I get into two to three conversations a day if I'm out there working in the garden, sharing produce or just spreading the word about growing your own food," he says. Credit: Kevin Espiritu

Credit: (opposite) Donna Griffith

Foodscaping is a word that has woven its way into the popular gardening lexicon, in parallel with edible landscaping. Rather than planting those typical rows of yore, the plants are worked into the design of the landscape, much like perennials. Texture, size, form, and color are all taken into consideration when planting both perennial and annual fruits and vegetables. Herbs can offer a great deal of diversity in terms of texture and leaf size—not to mention flavor. Look to add different varieties of sage, lemon thyme, parsley, and mint to container arrangements in place of other common "fillers."

Of course, there are benefits to planting food and flowers together. Not only will the plantings look nice from the curb, you'll attract valuable pollinators and other beneficial insects to your garden.

Sneak edibles into a front yard perennial garden.
Credit: Donna Griffith

For small-space gardeners, who might once have thought a bountiful harvest was out of reach, there are now many compact varieties of food plants available that can allow them to grow edibles in pots or smaller gardens. Keep an eye out for climbers, like cucumbers, watermelon, and beans, and tried-and-true favorites, tomatoes and peppers. These special plant varieties will not take over a space. And, there's no need to worry about a squash plant snaking its way through your garden to the neighbor's house. (Though that sometimes happens with my neighbor's plants, and I don't mind the unexpected harvest!)

Most food plants are also very ornamental in nature. Think about what they add to a garden in terms of color, flowers, foliage, and texture. Fennel adds a beautiful, fluffy texture to a garden. Speaking of texture, I've even seen asparagus being used as a hedge—after the spring harvest when the plant goes wild!

Think about other places you can sneak in food where flowers might have once ruled. Add a strawberry plant with red flowers to a hanging basket rather than a flowering annual. Even the fruit of some pepper plant varieties, like Mad Hatter and Dragon Roll, a shishito pepper, almost look like Christmas ornaments when they're dripping with peppers waiting to ripen.

This chapter is one that's near and dear to my heart because, in speaking about front yard veggie gardens, I get to delve into one of my favorite topics: raised beds. This ties into my last book, *Raised Bed Revolution*, because there are some raised bed projects both big and small that work really well in a front yard garden.

Growing food is a great way to taste new varieties and cross summer items off your grocery list—when you get to "shop" for them in your own yard. Whether your front yard is big or small, be on the lookout for inspiration and clever projects for your veggies.

SNEAKING VEGGIES INTO SIDE YARDS

An episode of *Big Dreams, Small Spaces* (episode 4, series 2), a BBC show featuring renowned green thumb and British TV presenter Monty Don, features neighbors on either side of a semidetached home who wanted to combine their two small front yard gardens.

A fence is knocked down and hardscaping is removed so one big shared garden is formed. The show adds a bit of suspense and drama as it seems both gardeners have their own ideas about what they want to see, but, ultimately, a plan is put in place and a beautiful front yard garden is created.

I was reminded of this episode when I discovered that friends from my book club, who also happen to be neighbors, share a veggie garden between their homes in their side yard and visible from the street . . .

Peek through the two houses and you discover a whimsical raised bed garden area that's seemingly smack dab in the middle of the property line. The garden (protected from four-legged pests) is shared by both families: the kids are in charge of planning and planting and, apparently, it's a friendly free-for-all when it comes to picking and enjoying the harvest.

Both moms agree that having a vegetable garden is a great learning tool for the kids. Right: The year before, one of the children won second prize in the kids/ youth category at the local fair for growing a prize-winning pumpkin. At the time this photo was taken, the kids from both houses have pumpkins planted and are crossing fingers they'll be prize winners, too! Credit: Donna Griffith

CHOOSING SOIL FOR YOUR VEGGIES

When putting together your front yard vegetable garden, depending on where you're planting, choose your soil accordingly. For an in-ground garden, amend the soil thoroughly with compost. Raised beds are usually built to solve the problem of having to garden in hard-packed, root-filled or clay soil. A soil delivery is likely the most cost-effective option to fill a raised bed. The company you order from will be able to calculate the amount, based on the depth and dimensions of your raised bed.

Where I live, triple mix, which includes top soil, peat moss or black loam, and compost are mixed to make vegetable garden soil. In the United States, 50/50 mix, which is top soil and compost, is generally what you'll find. Don't be afraid to ask questions to help you choose the best-quality soil for growing your veggies.

For small raised beds and containers, choose a potting soil formulated for growing vegetables. This mix actually contains no soil. It's lighter weight and more aerated than garden soil, which will promote better drainage in pots than a much heavier garden soil. The components of bagged potting soil (some green thumbs mix their own) usually include sphagnum peat moss or coir, perlite, compost, and an organic fertilizer that give plants a head start. You might still want to add some compost to it, for extra nutrients.

In fall, when putting the gardens to bed, if using smaller pots (especially if they're terracotta or ceramic), you may want to discard the soil and put them away for the winter. If they're larger containers, like paint buckets, you may not want to go to the effort of refilling them again, so you can amend the soil with compost in fall and/or spring. Amend the soil in raised beds in fall and/or spring with compost and/or leaf mold.

A LIGHTWEIGHT, LOW-COMMITMENT CONTAINER OPTION

If you're not sure about giving over your whole front yard garden to vegetable production, consider less permanent options. It's recommended that you start small, so you can assess how much work it takes to maintain one raised bed or a collection of pots.

Fabric raised beds are a great invention because they can be easily moved, they can be placed anywhere, and, if you do want to get rid of the soil in fall (this would be for smaller-size fabric pots), you can shake them out, fold them up, and put them away for winter.

Fabric raised beds come in many sizes, both round and square, big and small. I have a big one where I plant melons and cucumbers—this one I don't empty. And, I have a smaller one in which I plant potatoes each year. This one is emptied and put away for the season after the plants are pulled and I've dug around for all the potatoes.

Fabric raised beds could be set up on a driveway or be used to fill a hole somewhere in an established garden, provided the light requirements are good.

Another bonus is that they're made of a permeable material, which allows for a process called air or root pruning to occur. As air moves through the soil and the fabric of the pot, it strengthens the roots, resulting in healthy plants.

DESIGN TIPS FOR INTERPLANTING EDIBLES WITH ORNAMENTALS

Whether planted in a garden or container, there are many fruits, vegetables, and herbs that have great ornamental qualities. In England, for example, I fell in love with fennel planted among lupins, adding that wispy, ethereal texture you see from ornamental grasses, and that is a popular look in urban meadows.

I'm intrigued by the idea of a row of compact blueberry bushes replacing a boxwood hedge. Perhaps it was having made a few too many impulse purchases at the local garden center, but, for a few years now, I've been tucking herbs, like sage, parsley, interesting basil varieties, and lemon thyme into my gardens and pots. Not only do they provide interesting foliage, they give off a lovely fragrance when I garden close by—and, of course, they're edible.

You don't need a massive vegetable garden to enjoy the taste of a homegrown tomato. Sneak one into your front yard perennial bed with a fancy obelisk and it becomes an ornamental plant.
Credit: Donna Griffith

Whether you have a small space or a perennial garden with a few strategically placed holes to fill, you can grow a rainbow of tomatoes in your front yard.
Credit: Tara Nolan

SNEAKING EDIBLES INTO YOUR ORNAMENTAL GARDEN

If you don't have the space to dig in a traditional vegetable garden with rows, or to install a raised bed or two, there are plenty of options that give green thumbs the opportunity to grow edibles. Sneak food plants into your ornamental garden among the perennials.

HERE ARE A FEW IDEAS:

1. Tomatoes don't just come in red. There is a rainbow of heirloom varieties—blue, purple, pink, orange—to discover, all with different flavor profiles. I discovered a delicious and eye-catching variety called Thai Pink Egg from a local tomato sale. The fruits are white as they grow and turn pale pink as they ripen.

2. Add an ornamental berry bush among other perennial plants and bushes. There are some lovely compact, self-pollinating varieties with yummy names, such as Pink Icing, Jelly Bean, and Pink Sorbet, which have very ornamental foliage with the added bonus of fruit.

Potted herbs bring beauty and form to any front yard or porch. Credit: Niki Jabbour

Lemongrass has many culinary uses and makes a lively spiked ornamental. Credit: Tara Nolan

3. Add height to your ornamental containers with lemongrass in place of a traditional *Dracaena* or spike. You can dry it for herbal tea and pull sprigs in fall to use in curries and other dishes.

4. Choose herbs, such as rosemary, parsley (both curly and flat-leaf), and mint (look for fun varieties, like mojito, apple, or chocolate) in place of traditional foliage plants to include in your summer container arrangements or to add to borders. (With the exception of mint. Never plant mint in the garden. You'll be pulling it out forever!)

5. Sneak kale and swiss chard into pots or anywhere in the garden that needs a bit of foliage. Experiment with different varieties, colors, and textures, like dinosaur kale or blue vates.

6. Plant a fruit tree in your front yard. Even on a small property you can select and plant a dwarf variety. It will blossom in spring, showing off beautiful flowers, provide fruit in summer (if birds or other critters don't beat you to it), and provide a nice autumn display.

7. Edge your flower garden with edible greens, like lettuces (though be mindful that you may have to pull out varieties that bolt in hot weather), mustard, or spinach.

8. Add pepper plants among your perennials. They're fairly compact plants with nice foliage, and the peppers add a pop of color to the garden. Even a nice habanero will look attractive as you wait for those hot peppers to ripen.

Dinosuar kale (also called Tuscan kale or lacinato kale) is a stunning front yard player. Credit: Niki Jabbour

Just about any kind of pepper plant, including this chile pepper plant, adds sparkle to a yardscape.
Credit: Niki Jabbour

Think about tucking a basil plant in among ornamental plants for fragrant foliage, or allow it to shine on its own. Credit: Niki Jabbour

9. Make a small hedge out of perennial herbs using sage or chives. Use them to encircle bulbs in spring, flowering annuals in summer, and annual mums in fall.

10. If you're looking to add a plant with height to the garden, dig in a columnar basil plant. You can harvest fresh leaves throughout the season to flavor summer dishes and when you're ready, cut the whole thing down to make pesto.

11. Add a trailing herb, such as oregano or lemon thyme, to your hanging baskets otherwise filled with colorful annuals. The edible foliage, like creeping Jenny, will act as a spiller instead of a traditional annual.

12. If you're short on space in your front yard, look for places where you can hang your veggies. Look for tomato varieties, like Tumbling Tom, that you can grow in a hanging basket.

13. Grow a small fruit tree or shrub in a container. Figs grow well in containers and can be brought inside to a cold room to over winter so they can go dormant.

Here, lemon thyme and Sanvitalia Powerbini have been used to edge the upper tier of a garden. The herbs can be trimmed to dry throughout the season, while offering visual interest in an ornamental bed. Credit: Donna Griffith

EDGE A GARDEN WITH EDIBLES

Edging a garden with veggies is the reverse of how I usually edge my raised beds. I'll plant flowers, like marigolds and alyssum, along the edges. If you have an established perennial garden, rather than edging it this year with flowering annuals, why not plant edible annuals instead? This is a great way to sneak food into an ornamental garden.

Amend the soil where you're going to plant with lots of compost, as you would a regular vegetable garden.

Think of interesting combos. In spring, lettuces don't mind the cool weather. You'll be able to harvest the outer leaves and let the inside leaves continue to grow—and fulfill their ornamental duties. Once the first heatwaves hit and the lettuce starts to bolt, you won't be able to eat the bitter leaves. If you'd like to plant more lettuce, wait until the end of summer. Or, plant heat-tolerant greens, like New Zealand spinach. Keep plants trimmed and small.

You can also experiment with an edge planting featuring herbs, such as lemon thyme, chives, spicy globe basil, or parsley.

COMPACT PLANTS: PERFECT SIZES FOR SMALL SPACES

Whether you have a free piece of driveway, a corner of a porch, or a small front garden, all these spaces can help you fulfill your green thumb dreams of picking fresh tomatoes off the vine or snipping salad for supper. The space needs at least six to eight hours of sun for most edibles to thrive (though there are some that don't mind shade). And, if you thought productive spreaders and climbers, like cucumbers, beans, and squash, were out of the question, there are solutions available. Look for compact plant varieties with the word "patio" on the seed packet or plant tag. Those are your best bets. In fact, there's a tomato variety that's simply called "Patio" tomato. But if you do a little searching, you'll find others, too.

COMPACT FRUIT

Now, let's talk about fruit. There are some fantastic varieties of edible berries you can plant in a pot or small garden. And a lot of them have ornamental qualities, so they have a dual purpose when you decide to display them in a front yard. Look for self-pollinating plants, like those sold by Bushel and Berry, a company that offers delicious-sounding varieties such as Pink Icing blueberry (I have this one; the foliage is gorgeous and changes throughout the seasons), Raspberry Shortcake (which is thornless), and Baby Cakes blackberry (a dwarf variety that is also thornless). There are also lots of great strawberry varieties, like Delizz, that do well in pots.

Delizz strawberry plant
Credit: Tara Nolan

Mardi Gras Fun Series
F1 Snack Pepper
Credit: Tara Nolan

Little Birdy tomato
Credit: Tara Nolan

Pink Icing blueberry
Credit: Bushel and Berry

COMPACT VEGGIE VARIETIES

TOMATOES

Baby Boomer
Better Bush
BushSteak
Inca Jewels
Litt'l Bites Cherry
Little Birdy
  (comes in
  yellow-red,
  yellow, and
  orange)
Sweet Valentines
Tasmanian
  Chocolate
Tidy Rose
Tidy Treats
Tiny Tim
Tumbling Tom
Window Box

CUCUMBER

Bush Slicer
Patio Snacker
Salad Bush

PEPPERS

Lemon Dream
Shishito
Tangerine Dream

PEAS

Lincoln Garden
Little Crunch
Little Marvel
Peas-in-a-Pot

CARROTS

Romeo
Short Stuff

EGGPLANT

Little Fingers
Patio Baby

BEANS

Mascotte
The "Weekend
  Bean"

**Dragon Roll
shishito pepper**
Credit: Tara Nolan

DRIVEWAY GARDENS

If there is an obstacle preventing you from having a backyard garden—perhaps you are short on space or a big old tree in your yard or your neighbor's yard is casting shade—the driveway may be the perfect spot to site a garden, provided you don't need all of said space for a car.

There are a few things to keep in mind. Summer sun on asphalt can get pretty hot, so the soil will dry out much more quickly. You also want to give your containers adequate drainage and be mindful of where all the runoff from watering goes. Speaking of runoff, be sure to set up a regular schedule for applying organic fertilizer to your pots (follow the package directions). Constant watering washes away nutrients that aren't being absorbed by the plant from the container.

Jazz up paint buckets like the ones you would get at a big box or hardware store with a burlap wrap. I found these burlap coffee bags at an antique market. Pin or sew the burlap in place along the back. Drill holes in the bottom of the containers for drainage.
Credit: Donna Griffith

Whether on the driveway or directly next to it, a raised bed (such as a stock tank) presents an opportunity to grow veggies where you otherwise could **not.** Credit: Paul Zammit

If space permits, line up your veggie garden (i.e. all your containers) on your driveway. Credit: Jennifer Wright

A self-contained raised vegetable bed can be snuck into a driveway garden landscape among perennials. This one, from Vegepod Australia, is self-watering and on a wheeled trolley stand, making it easy to roll wherever you get the sun and then into storage for winter. It's also nice and accessible for humans and less accessible for pests, like rabbits. Credit: Vegepod Australia

I have run into many folks who have found ways to utilize their unused driveway space for growing gardens. Here is a helpful look at a couple.

Jennifer Wright plants all her vegetables in pots on her driveway. Her house is adjacent to the Niagara Escarpment, which means the forest edge—and the resident hungry animals—are her neighbors. She learned this the hard way when she first bought her home more than five years ago. Everything she planted in the ground was gobbled up by the local deer and rabbits. Determined not to give up, she turned to planting in pots on the driveway, thinking the animals wouldn't be so bold as to get that close to the house. She was right.

"Having all my vegetables in pots in my driveway allows me to enjoy them more," says Jennifer. "I see them several times a day (i.e., on my way in to work and when I get home each day), which gives me the chance to watch them carefully and water often." Jennifer grows tomatoes, kale, spinach, leaf lettuce, swiss chard, brussels sprouts, broccolini, peppers, cucumbers, snap peas, and chives. Her main advice is: to be successful growing vegetables in pots, invest in the best soil!

Despite growing many pots of vegetables in her driveway, Jennifer still has room to park her car. Credit: Jennifer Wright

For the past couple of seasons, garden writers **Steven Biggs** and his daughter, **Emma**, have set up straw bales on their urban driveway. The main goal was to make tomato-growing space for Emma because it's her passion and much of the yard is unsuited to tomatoes because of a black walnut tree next door.

The straw bales contain tomatoes and peppers, with a few eggplants, greens, and cucumbers. The water soaks into and through the bales the same way it would soil. By fall, the straw has decomposed considerably—and makes a great mulch for the other garden beds.
Credit: Steven Biggs

BUILDING WITH FRONT YARD VEGETABLE GARDENING IN MIND

Two raised beds in this front yard are as stalwart as the trees behind them. And obviously, they're taking advantage of the best spot in the yard for sunlight. They have been leveled on a subtle slope.
Credit: bufco.ca

There are a lot of creative DIY possibilities for front yard food gardening, but the most popular is raised beds.

There was a time when it would have been very unusual to see raised beds in a front yard garden. Vegetable gardens have long been relegated to the backyard. But in the past several years, it's become much more common to see front yard vegetable gardening increase in popularity while concerns about growing vegetables in this prime location diminish.

Often, it's the backyard's condition that drives homeowners to the front yard or driveway. Vegetables need at least six to eight hours of sunlight a day to thrive. And studies have shown you can more than double your yield per square foot (square meter) by planting in a raised bed compared to that standard, in-ground vegetable garden once relegated to a corner of the back yard.

Raised beds can be built to whatever size you need to suit your space. If you don't have the tools or woodworking skills, look at options like upcycled stock tanks or kits that come with all the materials, including nails and screws, that you assemble. Tools can always be borrowed.

There's something about stonework that elevates the look of any raised bed garden. Here, food and flowers enjoy the sun. Credit: bufco.ca

LIVE-EDGE RAISED BED

DESIGNED AND BUILT BY MARCEL CAMPOSILVAN
PHOTOS BY DONNA GRIFFITH
ILLUSTRATIONS BY LEN CHURCHILL

TOOLS

Straightedge (or chalk line)

Square

Circular saw

Spring clamp or similar

Drill

Orbital sander

Paintbrush (if staining)

Eye protection

Gloves

Ear protection

MATERIALS

2 pieces live-edge wood (enough for two sides at 35" [88.9 cm] and two sides at 20" [50.8 cm]); height varies between 8 and 14" (20.3 and 35.6 cm) because of the live edge

About 12¾" (32.4 cm) conventional #8 deck screws

Oil finish (this project used Behr Premium Transparent Penetrating Oil Wood Finish)

R aised beds are a great way to organize a vegetable garden in a front yard. And, sometimes, the front or driveway or side yard is the best location on your property to grow food, especially if your backyard is shady. You can get creative with the design, plant a lovely mix of food and flowers, and impress your neighbors with produce (if you have enough to share).

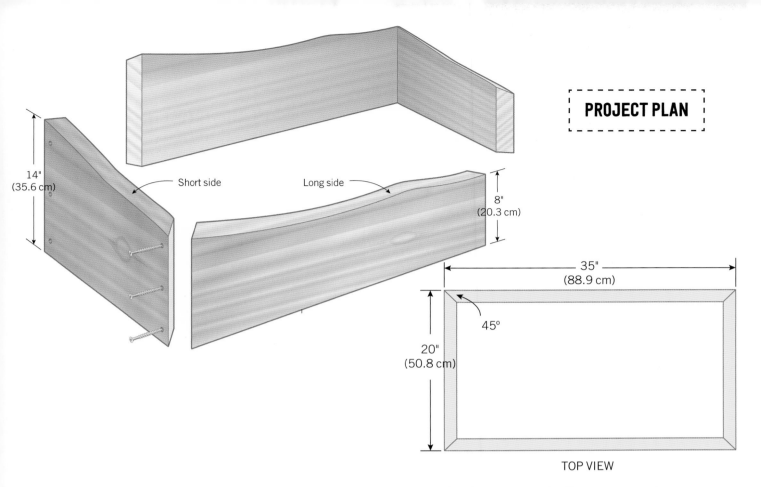

14"
(35.6 cm)

Short side

Long side

8"
(20.3 cm)

35"
(88.9 cm)

45º

20"
(50.8 cm)

TOP VIEW

Wherever they're located, there are multiple benefits to growing in raised beds. The soil warms up sooner in springtime, meaning you can get plants in the ground earlier, and you can easily rotate crops and plant families. If you're concerned about hard-packed or clay soil, you are able to control all the rich organic matter you put into a raised bed (or container). That soil also remains nice and loose and friable because you can easily reach into the garden from the sides to plant, weed, and harvest, rather than walking through the raised bed, which can compact the soil.

An added bonus? A study that came out of The Dawes Arboretum revealed that gardening in a raised bed produced double the yield of veggies grown in a traditional, in-ground garden of the same square footage.

If you are concerned about the size of a traditional raised bed, don't think you need to build it to 3 × 6' or 4 × 8' (0.9 × 1.8 m or 1.2 × 2.4 m). You can customize your raised bed to whatever size or height you need. You can still squeeze a lot of food into a smaller raised bed. Higher raised beds are great for those who have trouble bending or kneeling.

This particular raised bed was the perfect size to place in an empty corner of my front yard garden. It has an ornamental quality to it because of the live-edge poplar that was used.

Back to the placement: This raised bed gets the perfect amount of sunlight. You want to make sure your raised bed site gets at least six to eight hours of sunlight a day, especially if you're growing heat-loving

veggies like tomatoes, melons, peppers, and cucumbers.

Slabs of live-edge wood were used to build this project and the corners were mitered to give it a seamless look. Soft wood, such as cedar, works best for this project. The outside was stained to maintain the appearance of the wood; however, if you're growing food, I recommend not staining the inside, as you don't want anything to leach into the soil.

If you're looking for other raised bed ideas, there are more project plans in *Raised Bed Revolution*. I also provide upcycling ideas that could work in a front yard, like an old washbasin and suitcase.

CHOOSING MATERIALS FOR RAISED BEDS

If you're building your own raised beds, big or small, it's recommended to use a rot-resistant, untreated wood, such as cedar, white oak, or hemlock. I used untreated cedar for all of my raised beds.

What's most readily available will likely depend on where you live. Ask your local lumberyard for their recommendations on which materials should last the longest. Look for the Forest Stewardship Council (FSC) stamp on your wood. This international certification and labeling system has to meet certain standards that promote responsible forest management and tracks the source of the wood.

Upcycling and finding a new use for old materials is great, but be mindful of what you choose. If you have pressure-treated lumber from an old deck or fence you've taken apart, or railroad ties, you might not want to use them to build a raised bed because there may still be chemicals in the wood that can leach into the soil in which you're growing food.

There are now eco-friendly pressure-treated wood options, but readers are encouraged to do their own research and use what they feel comfortable with.

For some upcycling wood projects, you can line the wood with plastic to protect both the wood from rotting and the soil (if, for example the wood has old paint or stain on it) from contamination. Never add plastic to the bottom of your garden, however, as you want to promote good drainage.

PUTTING IT TOGETHER

For this project, instead of just nailing the boards together, the corners were mitered. In speaking to builder Marcel Camposilvan, the mitered corners are a traditional way to make a corner with two pieces of wood. "In this case, it really shows off the grain in the live edge because the grain can be matched making a 'waterfall' effect."

The ends of each length and width were cut straight with the circular saw before being mitered. Use a square to measure.

----

1. To start, square the wood to minimize any spalding or difficulty cutting the miter. Do this with care to make sure the same side of the wood faces the outside when you line up the corners to attach them.

----

2. Clamp the wood to your work table and, using a circular saw set to cut at 45°, carefully cut each miter. Predrill the wood to see how the corners will match. This is an essential step in keeping the corners lined up for assembly. With all the miters and the variances of a live edge piece of wood, trimming will sometimes be needed to nicely align each corner.

----

3. Drill all sides in place, using 3 screws per side. In this case, they were drilled from the short side of the raised bed so you cannot see them from the front.

----

4. Preserve the outside of the wood with an oil finish, if you wish. If you are going to add a finish, it's recommended that you only paint the outside of the raised bed and not the inside, as you don't want the finish leeching into the soil.

Cut two pieces to 35" (88.9 cm) each and two pieces to 20" (50.8 cm).

Measure the wood to figure out which parts of the live edge you'll use.

Drill all sides in place, using three screws per side.

ADDING A RAISED BED TO A SLOPE IN A FRONT YARD

Not all front yards are flat. In fact, most should slope away from the home, so it would look very peculiar if you just plunked a rectangular raised bed on a sloped piece of land. But there is a clever way to work with the slope, so you can work with your grade and build accordingly.

My friends Marc Green and Arlene Hazzan Green of BUFCO, a company that makes raised bed kits, including these wonderful raised beds that are wheelchair accessible, shared their method for measuring your slope before installing a raised bed. These guidelines will also help determine the height of the bed.

You'll want to be mindful of the soil on your property. A taller raised bed is great for areas that have really poor compacted or clay soil, or soil strewn with roots. If the native soil underneath where you want to site your raised bed is healthy, with a nice friable texture, you can get away with a shallower raised bed.

If your property is gently sloped away from the home, you might be able to get away with a shorter raised bed. But if the grade is steeper, you'll want your dimensions to accommodate a taller raised bed.

The important point that Marc makes is to make sure your raised bed is level with the horizon—and that you don't eyeball it. Not only will it blend in with the landscape better this way, but if it's on an angle, you risk having plants and seeds washed away in a heavy rain.

You'll only be leveling the footprint of the sides of the raised bed, where the bed walls touch the ground. You don't need to level the footprint of the entire raised bed, unless you are concerned about the existing soil (compacted, poor soil health, roots, etc.).

TOOLS

Tape measure with locking mechanism

Tent peg or sturdy stick to push into the ground

String (10 to 12' [3 to 3.7 m])

Longer stick (i.e., bamboo), no more than 24" (61 cm)

Line level (a.k.a. string level) with two little hooks from which you can hang the level on the string

Measuring your grade will help you determine if your front yard is sloped or flat.

Note: The measurements in this project are made based on a 4 × 8' (1.2 × 2.4 m) raised bed. They also assume there's a grade to the area and that you want the 8' (2.4 m) of length to be placed along the slope. Other options to overcome a sloped installation site include taller beds to compensate for the grade; turning the bed 90 degrees so the 4' (1.2 m) wall runs along the grade, which will basically cut the height of the grade in half; or live with less exposed height at the top of the grade.

This will all depend on site dimensions and personal preference. There are still a lot of important considerations to make before you install your raised beds, but now that you can measure your grade accurately, you've taken care of one of the most important ones.

You'll be using your string with a line level to figure out the difference between the high part of the grade and the low part of the grade, across the 8' (2.4 m) span where your bed will sit.

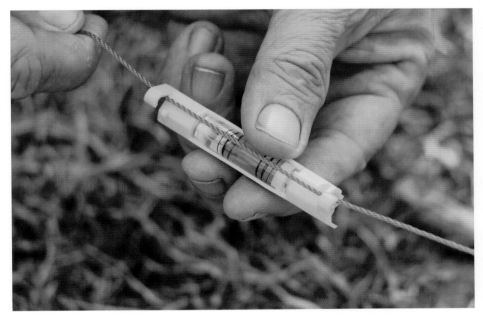

A line level in use.
Credit: bufco.ca

STEPS FOR INSTALLING A RAISED BED ON A SLOPE

1. Use your measuring tape to measure out the 8' (2.4 m) length of your garden bed. Lay the tape on the ground.

2. Insert the tent peg at the high end of the grade and tie the string to it. Push the peg right into the ground so the string touches the top of the soil (or the base of the grass).

3. Take the string down to the other end of the tape measure. Push the tall stake into the ground at the 8' (2.4 m) mark. This marks where the bed ends.

4. Now that both ends of the bed are marked, retrieve the tape measure.

5. Position yourself at the bottom of the grade, next to the tall stake, and hang the line level on the string.

6. Raise and lower the string until the air bubble in the level is right in the middle. The string is now level to the horizon.

7. Using the tape measure, note the distance between the top of the soil and the string. The number at the string line is the differential between the highest part of the grade and the lowest part of the grade over the 8' (2.4 m) length of your garden bed.

It can sometimes be tricky to hold the string just so in one hand and the extended tape measure in the other hand while trying to get an accurate reading. If that's the case, tie the string to the bamboo stake in the exact level position. Or, draw a line with a marker on the stake at the exact level position. Now, you've got both hands available to manipulate the tape measure. Either way, make sure the string is level. And, it never hurts to measure twice.

ANOTHER OPTION FOR FIGURING OUT A SLOPE

Get yourself an 8' (2.4 m) length of 2 × 4 wood. Make sure it's straight and true, otherwise it could mess up your measurements. Tape a level to the wood, and place it along the 8' (2.4 m) path where you're going to install your bed. Let one end of the 2 × 4 rest on the highest point on the install area. Lift the other end—the low end—until the bubble in the level is centered. Use your measuring tape to measure the distance from the ground to the bottom of the wood. That's the grade over the 8' (2.4 m) install area, the difference between the high ground and the low ground over the length your 8' (2.4 m)-long bed. Note that the string method tends to be more accurate.

Once you know your grade, it's time for some simple math. In this example, the grade along the 8' (2.4 m) length of the bed is 9" (22.9 cm). That means, at the high end of the grade the bed walls will be buried 9" (22.9 cm) into the ground, and the low end of the bed will be "at grade"— sitting on top of the ground and not buried.

You will lose 9" (22.9 cm) of bed height to the grade. If you were planning on installing a raised bed that's 16" (40.6 cm) tall, it'll be 16" (40.6 cm) tall at the low end, but only 7" (17.8 cm) tall at the high end. That's 9" (22.9 cm) below grade and 7" (17.8 cm) above grade. With so much of the bed buried, you may want to consider a taller bed. If you move to a 24" (61 cm)-tall bed, you'll have all that height exposed at the low end and a pretty comfy 15" (38.1 cm) exposed at the high end.

A 16" (40.6 cm)-tall bed can deal with a 2 to 3" (5.1 to 7.6 cm) grade nicely. Once you start getting steeper than that, you might want to consider a taller bed. If you stick with the 16" (40.6 cm) bed on a significant grade, you'll still get most of the benefits of a raised bed, but you will sacrifice some of the above-ground height that helps bring the garden up to you.

Melissa J. Will grew both food and flowers on a front lawn measuring 8' (2.4 m) wide. Credit: Melissa J. Will

HOW A GARDENER CAME OUT AS A FRONT YARD VEGETABLE GROWER

If you're a little nervous about taking the leap into front yard veggie growing, especially if the garden is conspicuously grown in a raised bed, Melissa J. Will of the wonderfully creative Empress of Dirt website might be able to put your mind at ease.

Melissa explains her fear of turning the front yard of her former home into a productive veggie garden. "Aware of the upper middle class stigma attached to front grass-free gardens and reluctant to face the protest of neighbors, I avoided removing the front lawn for years, even though it was the only full-sun area I had," she says.

Melissa's desire to grow vegetables eventually overpowered her fears, resulting in a raised bed, followed by two more. With trepidation she waited for complaints that never materialized. In fact, she met new neighbors who were interested in the garden and asked questions.

ROLLING VERSAILLES-INSPIRED PLANTER

DESIGNED AND BUILT BY SCOTT MCKINNON
PHOTOS BY DONNA GRIFFITH
ILLUSTRATIONS BY LEN CHURCHILL

TOOLS

Bevel square or carpenter's square and a pencil

Miter saw

Hammer or pneumatic nailer

Sand paper or rounding plane

MATERIALS

1 sheet ³/₄" (1.9 cm) exterior plywood

1 box 1¹/₂" (3.8 cm) exterior screws

1 set of 4 (2¹/₂", or 6.4 cm) casters

12 (10' [3 m] long × 1³/₄" [4.4 cm] wide) cedar strips

1 box finishing nails

PROJECT PLAN

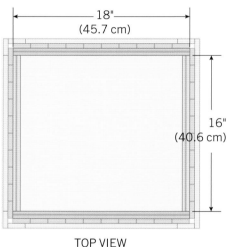

18" (45.7 cm)

16" (40.6 cm)

TOP VIEW

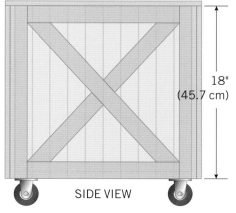

18" (45.7 cm)

SIDE VIEW

I like the regal look of the Versailles planters you see when strolling the grounds of France's most famous palace. The original was designed in 1670 by André Le Nôtre, King Louis XIV's gardener. These portable containers were built for the orange trees that were imported to the castle, so it would be easy to move them into l'orangerie, the property's greenhouse, for the winter. Though the main photo shows off a highbush blueberry, it turned into a summer home for my 'Verte' fig tree.

Locking wheels make it easy to roll this lovely box into the garage in fall (when I take the fig tree out and bring it indoors to go dormant for the winter in a cold room) and back outdoors in spring.

Hinged doors and finials were the finishing touches on the original model, which had a cast iron frame. In this project, cedar strips were rounded using a rounding plane to create the X pattern and wheels were attached to the bottom to make it easy to roll into and out of storage.

I used an outdoor stain to protect the wood on the inside and outside from the elements. It was red when it was first built and is now navy to match my wooden chairs. Because my plant is in a pot, I don't worry about the stain leaching into the soil in which it's growing. I wouldn't paint the inside if I planted directly into the container.

Top strips

Wide side panels

Narrow side panels

Narrow side panel

Wide side panel

Side corner strips

Caster

Side corner strip

Vertical cedar strips

Horizontal strip

Short diagonal strip

Long diagonal strip

If you are looking to place a tree in this container, you can increase the dimensions to hold it. The pot of my fig tree is about 14" (35.6 cm) in diameter. Because of its reasonable size, this planter would allow someone with a small space to grow a fig tree or berries, such as blueberries, strawberries, or blackberries (see "Compact Plants: Perfect Sizes for Small Spaces").

PUTTING IT TOGETHER

1. Cut two pieces of plywood 18×18" (45.7×45.7 cm) for side pieces, and two pieces of plywood $18 \times 16^1/2$" (45.7×41.9 cm) for the other side pieces. Cut one piece of plywood $16^1/2 \times 16^1/2$" (41.9×41.9 cm) for the bottom. Assemble the plywood box with the smaller sides inside the larger ones and the bottom panel enclosed on all sides. Attach the pieces with screws.

2. Cut 48 pieces of cedar strip to 18" (45.7 cm) each. Lay 10 pieces out per side, nailing them on vertically with finishing nails.

3. With a rounding plane or sandpaper, round the long edges of all the cedar strips. The one used for this project could be used on the push or the pull stroke, creating the desired effect in one or two passes. This gives them a nice curved finish.

4. To make a side corner, place two strips perpendicular to each other so each piece meets evenly at the corner of the box. They'll form an L shape. Nail the strips tight. Repeat for all the other corners.

5. Measure for the horizontal strips that run between the corner pieces along the top and the bottom.

Profile the edges of the strips with a rounding plane.

Locking wheels make it easy to roll this planter into storage for winter.

MAKE HEAVY CONTAINERS "PORTABLE"

If you have any wooden planters (with a sturdy bottom) you wish you could more easily move around your property, casters are very easy to find at big box stores. They can be attached with screws (predrill the holes using a $1/4$" [6 mm] wood bit) and fastened firmly in place with a nut and bolt. Similarly, you could create a small "dolly" out of wood and casters and place pots on it to move them around.

Note: Lapping the corners as was done in the previous step could alter the measurements of these pieces a little. Measure them before cutting. Attach these 8 strips (top and bottom on all 4 sides) by nailing them in place.

6. To make the top edge of the planter, take a longer piece of cedar and measure the inside lengths of the planter. This is the measurement you want so you can cut two opposing 45-degree angles on either end so all the pieces meet evenly in the corners. Continue to measure and cut all the way around. Nail everything in place.

7. Lay a piece from corner to corner and line it up how you want it in the corners. With a pencil, mark the angled cut you'll need to make it fit. It should be 45 degrees, or very close, depending on how you've laid out the box. For the crosspiece, mark where it will need to be cut out in the center so the two pieces fit snugly around the other half of the X. Repeat for all sides.

MINI LETTUCE/ HERB TABLE FOR A FRONT PATIO

DESIGNED BY TARA NOLAN
BUILT BY TARA NOLAN AND BILL NOLAN
PHOTOS BY DONNA GRIFFITH
ILLUSTRATION BY LEN CHURCHILL

TOOLS

Tape measure

Handsaw or miter saw

Tin snips or wire cutters for real hardware cloth; scissors for plastic version

Heavy-duty stapler

Nail gun and air compressor or impact driver

Eye and ear protection

Work gloves

MATERIALS

One 2 × 4" (5.1 × 10.2 cm) cedar board

Cedar deck screws

Painter's tape

Roll hardware cloth (can cut to size for finished project)

One 1 × 2" × 10' (2.5 × 5.5 cm × 3 m)

One 1 × 6" × 5' (2.5 × 15.2 cm × 1.5 m) cedar fence board

Sandpaper

Wood glue

Oil finish (optional)

T here's something fun and challenging about trying to squeeze as many herbs and veggies as possible into a small space. Pinterest can send you down a rabbit hole of fun and creative ideas. For this project, I decided to downsize my lettuce table design from *Raised Bed Revolution* to create a side table that would fit a selection of leafy greens (lettuces, spinach, pea shoots, baby kale, etc.), or perhaps a small selection of herbs.

I thought I might find an old side table to convert, like I had with the small kitchen table in the original project, but I came away empty-handed from a trip to a couple of antique markets. I put my thinking cap back on and decided to design my own simple table. It had two requirements: to accommodate planting those leafy greens and to be able to hold a tea cup—or wine glass, whatever your preference!

Lettuce only needs a depth of about 3 to 4" (7.6 to 10.2 cm) to grow, so you can get away with a much shallower garden, than for, say, a tomato (even one that's patio size!). The table should be high enough that garden pests, like your resident rabbit, shouldn't be able to get into it, but low enough to hold a couple of summer cocktails on fancy coasters between a couple of comfy chairs.

If you were to happen upon an old side table with an easy-to-remove top, turn it over, staple hardware cloth to the bottom frame, add cedar strips, if necessary as extra reinforcement and to cover the edges, and voilà. You've essentially created a basket with wooden sides. Read on to learn how to make your own.

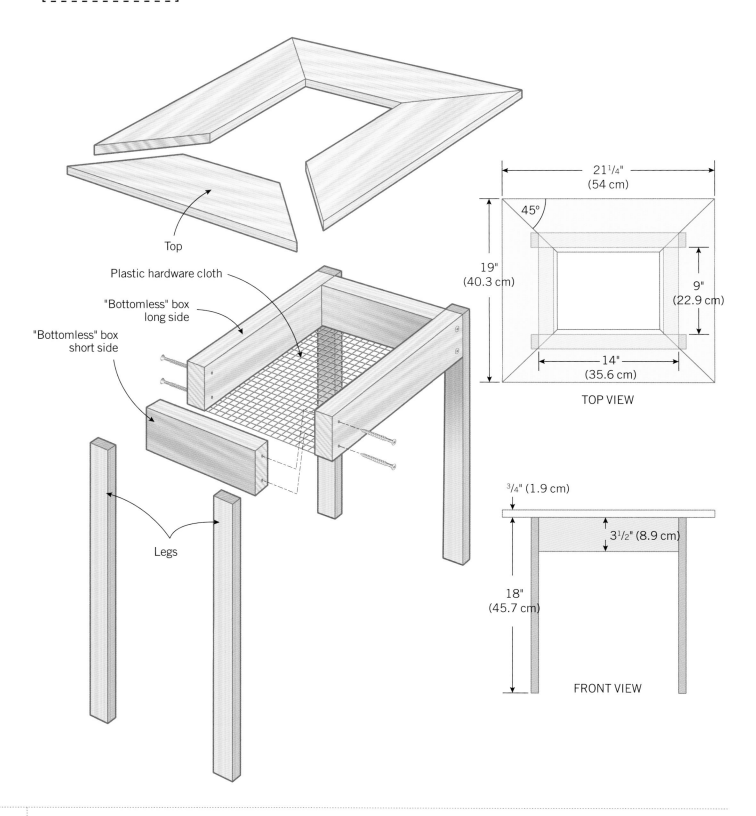

Top

Plastic hardware cloth

"Bottomless" box long side

"Bottomless" box short side

Legs

21¹/₄"
(54 cm)

45°

19"
(40.3 cm)

9"
(22.9 cm)

14"
(35.6 cm)

TOP VIEW

³/₄" (1.9 cm)

3¹/₂" (8.9 cm)

18"
(45.7 cm)

FRONT VIEW

When your project is complete, line your "basket" with landscape fabric and fill with soil.

PUTTING IT TOGETHER

1. Cut the 2 × 4" (5.1 × 10.2 cm) into four pieces: two pieces at 9" (22.9 cm) each and two pieces at 14" (35.6 cm). These will form the "basket." Use deck screws to affix the long ends to the short ends to form a rectangular frame.

2. Using painter's tape, tape the edge of the roll of hardware cloth (I found this to be an easy way to keep the plastic hardware cloth in place). Stretch it to the other end of the rectangular frame and tape it in place. Using the stapler, staple the cloth around all the outside edges. This will form the bottom of your basket.

Use stainless steel staples to attach your hardware cloth to the bottom of your "basket."

3. Cut the $1 \times 2"$ (2.5×5.1 cm) into four 18" (45.7 cm) pieces. These will be the legs. Use a nail gun to attach them to the short sides of the table, as shown. I used a nail gun because it doesn't leave big holes, but you could also use fancy deck screws.

4. Cut the cedar fence board into two $21^3/_{16}"$ (53.8 cm) pieces and two $18^5/_{16}"$ (46.5 cm) pieces. This makes it easy to square up the top with a $^1/_4"$ (6 mm) overhang on the inside when you lay it over the base.

5. Using the miter saw, make 45-degree cuts to the end of each piece so they all fit together like a picture frame. Sand the edges.

6. Use a heavy-duty wood glue for outdoor use to glue the frame together; then, if you don't want to mar the top of your table with nails, you can also glue the frame to the basket.

7. If you want to preserve the wood, staple plastic along the inside edges. Don't add any plastic to the bottom, as you want the water to be able to drain out. You can also add a coat of oil finish to the outsides of the table and legs. Avoid adding finish to the inside of the basket, as you don't want it to leach into the soil where you'll be planting.

Tip: If you lightly water your lettuce, it won't drip too much, but you can place a tray underneath, if necessary. You also might have to water more than once a day.

Cut away the extra hardware cloth. For an extra barrier to hold it in place, use small finishing nails to add cedar strips over top. This is also a good step if you're using metal hardware cloth and not the plastic because the cedar strips will protect the sharp edges.

WHAT IS HARDWARE CLOTH?

The name "hardware cloth" is deceiving because it resembles a wire mesh more than cloth. It usually comes in a roll and has a finer, square "weave," if you will, than a chicken wire, which has bigger round holes. The wire is quite strong. There is also a plastic version on the market that I found to be easier to work with and you don't have to worry about cutting your fingers on the edges. It cuts quite easily.

GREENS TO GROW

I love that lettuces are referred to as "cut and come again." This means you don't just pull out the lettuce at the roots. Rather, you snip the outer leaves, as needed, and allow the center to keep growing. Here are some of my favorite varieties:

Bergam's Green

Butterhead

Navara

Queen of Crunch Crisphead

Red Sails

Also consider planting fun greens like baby bok choi, baby kale, pea shoots, sunflower shoots, and other microgreens.

GARDEN OBELISK

BUILT BY BILL NOLAN AND RANDY MUIRHEAD
PHOTOS BY DONNA GRIFFITH
ILLUSTRATIONS BY LEN CHURCHILL

TOOLS

Tape measure

Pencil

Saw (handsaw, jigsaw, or circular)

Carpenter's square

Clamps

Drill

Drill bits including a countersink bit

Eye and ear protection

Work gloves

MATERIALS

Four 2 × 2" × 8' (5.1 × 5.1 cm × 2.4 m) boards

Three 1 × 2" × 8' (2.5 × 5.1 cm × 2.4 m) boards

One pound 2" (5.1 cm)

One pound 2½" (6.4 cm) deck screws

Eight 4d galvanized finish nails

1 finial

Outdoor paint (optional)

There are many ways to grow food and flowers vertically, but the obelisk is a garden classic. In a front yard, you might typically find one supporting some gorgeous flowering annual or perennial. But the stately, classy obelisk is a great way to sneak food plants into a traditional perennial garden.

In the backyard, you might feel okay with using more basic supports, like stakes and twine—I've seen people use hockey sticks to stake tomatoes—or those standard metal tomato cages that get all bent out of shape each year the moment you try to stick them in the ground. But there's something more sophisticated about a painted wooden obelisk.

If you don't have a DIY project in you, there are a great many obelisk styles, both new and antique, that will add impact to a front yard garden. They are often a sturdy wrought iron with some type of flourish—unless you're looking simply at the humble tomato cage. But back to the wooden variety—they are usually a nice triangular shape, tapered at the top and sometimes capped with a fancy finial. Look for wooden finials crafted to go on fence posts.

This obelisk looks fancy, but only requires three tools to build it: a saw, a drill, and a carpenter's square. There is a bit of adjusting required to get the top to line up well. Depending on the length of the 2 × 2" (5.1 × 5.1 cm) pieces of wood, adjust the height to whatever you need it to be. This project stands at 72" (182.9 cm) tall without the finial. You can shorten it according to your preference. We left a bit of length to be able to anchor the obelisk in the ground.

Do choose a rot-resistant wood, like hemlock or cedar. Your new favorite elegant garden accessory will last longer, allowing you to place it where it's needed in the garden from year to year. This one was also given a coat of outdoor paint. Its home is in a side yard, visible from the street, where it's holding up some unruly raspberry canes.

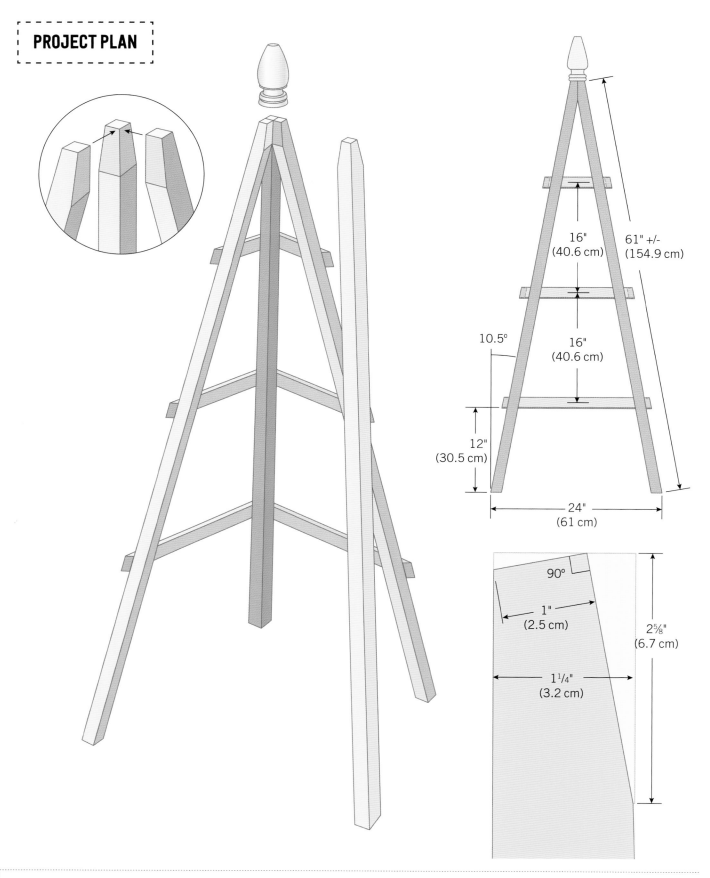

16"
(40.6 cm)

61" +/-
(154.9 cm)

10.5°

16"
(40.6 cm)

12"
(30.5 cm)

24"
(61 cm)

90°

1"
(2.5 cm)

2⁵⁄₈"
(6.7 cm)

1¹⁄₄"
(3.2 cm)

PUTTING IT TOGETHER

1. Measure the top of each leg. Mark the tops of the four legs for trimming. Each leg top should be trimmed so it has two beveled faces that meet in a point; then, trim them to length. Using a carpenter's square, mark a wedge shape on two adjoining faces at the top. The wedge should be 1" (2.5 cm) wide at a point 5" (12.7 cm) down from the top of the leg. Then, using a straight-edge, extend all four lines all the way to the edge of the workpiece. This will create two wedge shapes between 6 and 7" (15.2 and 17.8 cm) long. The old adage of measure twice and cut once applies here, as it can be a tricky process.

2. Using a handsaw, cut off one of the wedges to create a wedge-shaped waste piece. Flip your workpiece a quarter turn and cut off the other wedge. To finish trimming the leg tops, make a crosscut that follows the two 1" (2.5 cm) cutting lines you drew. This will leave a top that is 1×1" (2.5×2.5 cm) and is angled so it will be level when the legs are equally spread out in the garden.

3. Make the other tops the same way. When you're finished, the four legs should fit together to form a flat 2×2" (5.1×5.1 cm) top with the leg bottoms 24" (61 cm) apart.

Use a carpenter's square to mark diagonal cutting lines at the tops of the legs.

An old-fashioned handsaw does as a good a job as a power tool for trimming the leg tops.

Assemble two leg pairs by joining two legs to two crosspieces.

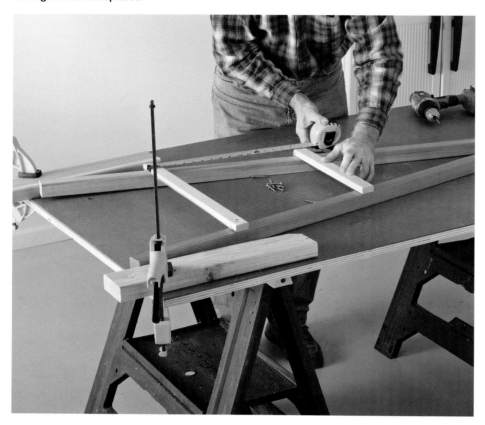

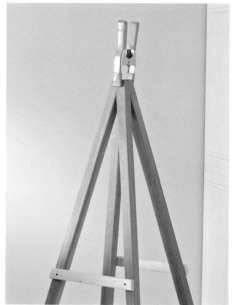

Stand the two assembled leg pairs upright with the tops joined together.

4. Make the leg frames. Space an obelisk leg pair 24" (61 cm) apart from outside to outside at the bottom and clamp or wedge them between two pieces of wood spaced to 24" (61 cm) apart. Cut a 1 × 2" (2.5 × 5.1 cm) to 22" (55.9 cm) long, lay it across the legs 12" (30.5 cm) from the bottom, and mark and cut the 1 × 2" (2.5 × 5.1 cm) flush with the legs. Fasten with 2" (5.1 m) screws driven through pilot holes. Cut and fasten another crosspiece 16" (40.6 cm) above the lower crosspiece (center to center). Join the tops of the 2 × 2" (5.1 × 5.1 cm) legs with a 2½" (6.4 cm) screw. Remove the assembled leg pair so you can repeat this step for the other two obelisk legs.

5. Use a clamp to hold the pieces together and space the legs 24" (61 cm) apart. Mark two more sets of crosspieces, this time cutting them flush with the 1 × 2s (2.5 × 5.1 cm). Fasten them to the 2 × 2s (5.1 × 5.1 cm) that are already installed, using screws driven through predrilled pilot holes. Screw the four tops together. If you want the 1 × 2s (2.5 × 5.1 cm) to match perfectly at the corners, make compound miter cuts on the ends. Trace the leg on a horizontal 1 × 2" (2.5 × 5.1 cm), then draw a 45-degree line from both the top and bottom of the line, connect them on the face of the 1 × 2" (2.5 × 5.1 cm), and cut that angle. Crosspieces can be placed according to preference.

6. Add the finial to the top. If you're using a standard finial from a home center, drill a hole for the integral lag screw in the center of the top and thread it in. If your finial doesn't come with an integral lag screw, nail and glue the finial to the tops of the posts.

7. Apply paint or stain to preserve the wood and make it stand out or blend in to the garden.

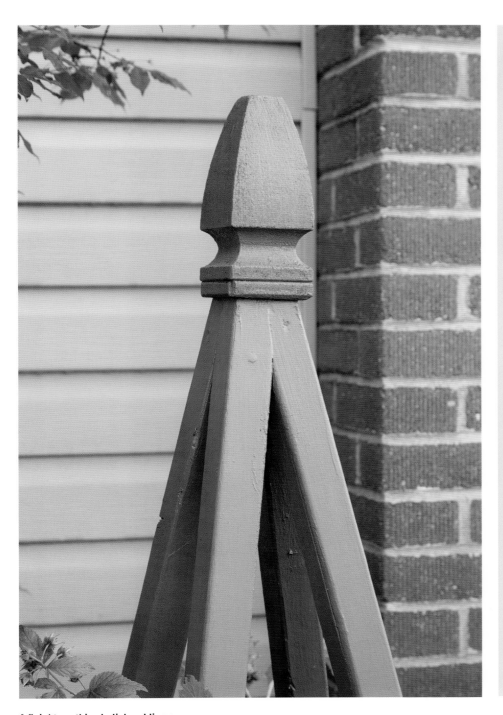

A finial tops this obelisk, adding a regal finish. Wood glue was used to attach it to the base and finishing nails were used to reinforce it further.

MODIFYING THE SIZE OF THE OBELISK

The obelisk in this project stands about 5' (1.5 m) tall, including the rounded finial on top. The base measures 24 × 24" (61 × 61 cm). The base for the finial has a diameter of 2¾" (7 cm), so the 2 × 2" (5.1 × 5.1 cm) posts both need to be 1" (2.5 cm) square at the top to provide a solid base and to cover the end grains.

The sides slope outward by 1' (30.5 cm) for every 5 vertical feet (1.5 m). You can alter the dimensions of your version by revising the numbers.

Simply divide the side of the obelisk into two right triangles. Half of the 24" (61 cm) base is 12" wide × 5' tall (30.5 cm × 1.5 m), which means it slopes 12" (30.5 cm) for every 5'. If you want your obelisk to be 3' wide × 6' tall (0.9 × 1.8 m), the slope changes to 1½' (0.5 m) for every 6' (1.8 m). Therefore, change the measurements on the square to 1½" (3.8 cm) and 6" (15.2 cm).

SAVE SPACE WITH A STAIRCASE PLANTER

PROJECT FROM *STEP-BY-STEP PROJECTS FOR SELF-SUFFICIENCY*

If you want to customize your stringers to match particular planters, use a framing square to calculate rise and run dimensions that will match your planters (see sidebar, page 140).

TOOLS

Framing square

Drill/driver

Tape measure

Hammer

Circular saw

Jigsaw (or handsaw)

Power miter saw (optional)

Countersink drill bit

Eye and ear protection

Work gloves

MATERIALS

Deck screws or exterior-grade self-tapping screws—1¼", 2", 3" (3.2 cm, 5.1 cm, 7.6 cm)

⁵⁄₁₆ × 3½" (8 mm × 8.9 cm) galvanized carriage bolts with washers and nuts

24" (61 cm)-long planter boxes

Large bag of potting mix or soil

2 × 10" × 8' (5.1 × 25.4 cm × 2.4 m) stock

2 × 4" × 12' (5.1 × 10.2 cm × 3.7 m) stock

2 × 6" × 8' (5.1 × 15.2 cm × 2.4 m) stock

1 × 2" × 8' (2.5 × 5.1 cm × 2.4 m) stock

For those who want to garden but have limited space, growing *up* is an easy answer. Vertical gardening can provide extra growing space if you need it or growing space in tight quarters.

This project could be placed anywhere—on a driveway, along a side yard, beside a fence. It provides about 7 square feet (0.65 m²) of planting space, but only takes up 2 square feet (0.19 m²) of actual space.

Another bonus? The area underneath the "steps" can be turned into valuable storage space for tools, watering cans, extra pots, etc.

Depending on the depth of the planters you purchase, you could plant anything from root veggies, like baby beets and globe carrots, to patio varieties of peppers, peas, and tomatoes. Of course, leafy greens, like lettuce, spinach, bok choy, and kale, and herbs, such as parsley, thyme, cilantro, and chives, would all thrive in a vertical salad garden, as well.

This project can be built on a budget using standard lumber and inexpensive planters. To simplify the work, use precut stair stringers sold at building centers. Typically used for deck stairs, the precut stringers are available with three to six risers, so you can choose the height that works best for you. Or, use standard stringer-cutting techniques to make your own custom stringers from outdoor-rated 2 × 10" (5.1 × 25.4 cm) lumber. To change the dimensions, adjust the rise, run, and distance between the stair stringers. You can also make the planter wider by adding additional stringers. You'll need a stringer about every 2 or 3' (0.6 to 0.9 m).

If you are making custom stringers, a full-size framing square will be your most valuable tool for this project.

OPTION: CUT YOUR OWN STRINGERS

If you choose to cut your own stringers to custom dimensions instead of buying precut stringers, start by measuring the planters you want to use and figuring out what your rise (height) and run (depth) need to be. Use a framing square to lay out the cutting lines on a piece of 2 × 10" (5.1 × 25.4 cm) exterior-rated lumber (top photo).

Start the cuts for each step with a circular saw and then finish them with a jigsaw or handsaw (right photo). Trim 1^1/$_2$" (3.8 cm) off the bottom of each stringer to allow for a 2 × 6" (5.1 × 15.2 cm) base plate.

PUTTING IT TOGETHER

1. Cut the 2 × 6" (5.1 × 15.2 cm) base plate for your planter. It should be the full planned width of the planter. Also from the 2 × 6" (5.1 × 15.2 cm), cut a spreader to fit between the stringers midway up. It should be 3" (7.6 cm) shorter than the base plate. And cut a third crosspiece for the top, 3" (7.6 cm) longer than the base plate.

2. Attach the middle crosspiece between the stringers along the back edges, midway from top to bottom, using 3" (7.6 cm) exterior-rated screws. Then, attach the base plate by screwing up through the plate and into the bottom of the stringers. The plate should extend ³/₄" (1.9 cm) past the fronts of the stringers to allow for the riser strips that will conceal the bottom opening. Attach the top crosspiece to the tops of the stringers at the back, flush with the top and overhanging each edge by 1¹/₂" (3.8 cm).

Attach the base plate, middle crosspiece, and top crosspiece to the stringers with 3" (7.6 cm) exterior-rated screws.

3. Make the leg assembly. This three-piece, U-shaped assembly captures the stringer assembly at the top and supports the structure. All parts are cut from 2 × 4" (5.1 × 10.2 cm) lumber. The height of the legs should equal the total planned height of the planter. Set the stringer on a flat surface with the base plate flat on the ground. Measure from the ground to the tops of the stringers. This is the required height of the legs. The 2 × 4" (5.1 × 10.2 cm) footer that connects the legs at the bottom should be precisely the same length as the top 2 × 6" (5.1 × 15.2 cm) crosspiece on the stringer assembly. Attach the footer to the backs of the legs with 3" (7.6 cm) screws.

4. Set the leg assembly upright on a flat surface and clamp the stringer assembly to it in position. The tops of the legs should be flush against the top crosspiece and level with the tops of the stringers. Drive 3" (7.6 cm) screws through the ends of the top crosspiece and into the backs of the leg tops.

Attach the leg assembly to the stringer assembly with 3" (7.6 cm) screws driven through the top crosspiece and into the legs.

5. Reinforce the connection between the leg assembly and the stringer assembly with two ⁵/₁₆ × 3¹/₂" (8 mm × 8.9 cm) galvanized carriage bolts per side. Drill guide holes for the carriage bolts and then drive them in so they are seated against the wood. Fasten them with washers and nuts to secure the joint.

6. Cut 1 × 2" (2.5 × 5.1 cm) filler strips to cover the first riser on the bottom of the planter, as well as the tops of the upper risers. These strips fill the visual gaps and also help stabilize the structure and prevent racking. Use 2" (5.1 cm) screws to attach the riser strips.

7. Apply any finish you choose. If you used cedar to make the planter, you can leave it untreated or coat it with a UV-resistant topcoating product. Pressure-treated lumber can be clear-coated, painted, or finished with deck stain.

8. Optional: If you are using plastic window boxes (recommended), put them in position on the stringers with the ends aligned. Secure them to the stringers with 1¹/₄" (3.2 cm) screws. Don't overdrive the screws.

SELF-WATERING PLANTERS

If your budget allows, look for self-watering planters. These are great options if you go away a lot in the summer and don't have anyone who can water in your absence. (They're also handy if you're a forgetful gardener.) Self-watering planters have a reservoir you fill so the planter can distribute the water consistently and evenly to the roots of the plant. All you have to do is make sure to check the reservoir every once in a while to ensure there is water in it.

WINDOW-WELL RAISED BED

DESIGNED AND BUILT BY TARA NOLAN
PHOTOS BY DONNA GRIFFITH
ILLUSTRATION BY LEN CHURCHILL

TOOLS

Table saw or miter saw

Drill/driver or impact driver

MATERIALS

Measurements are to fit a 41" (104.1 cm) window well

1 corrugated steel window well

One 1 × 12" (2.5 × 30.5 cm) cut to 41" (104.1 cm)

Twelve 2" (5 cm) screws

When I give my raised bed talk to garden clubs and horticultural societies, I display an image of two narrow raised beds made of painted corrugated steel placed in a side yard. More than one person has told me they look like two window wells attached. I love the look of corrugated steel, so that got me thinking . . . what if I bought two window wells and joined them together to make a raised bed?

I quickly discovered that the window well edges (at least on the examples I found at a local big box store) would not really attach easily and seamlessly. But, as I stood there trying to figure out what to do, I thought to myself, "What if I could attach one window

well to a piece of wood, to make sort of a semi-circular raised bed?" Wandering back to the lumber, I discovered that one metal window well was the exact height of a piece of a 1 × 12" (2.5 × 30.5 cm) piece of wood!

As noted in the Live-Edge Raised Bed project (page 114), gardening in raised beds offers green thumbs a variety of benefits (extended growing season, accessibility, overcoming roots and compact or poor soil, etc.). And, the great thing about raised beds is you can build them to be whatever size works with your space. I figured the narrow shape of this raised bed would fit perfectly in my side yard garden between my garage windows, where the

soil is very poor, despite my best efforts to amend it, and bindweed grows with abandon, despite my best efforts to tame it.

My side yard garden gets a LOT of sun, so veggies thrive there. You can place your window well raised bed anywhere that gets six to eight hours of sun per day (less if you plant veggies that don't mind a bit of shade, like greens—lettuce, spinach, etc. and beets). My first season growing in this garden, I dug in three pepper plants that absolutely flourished.

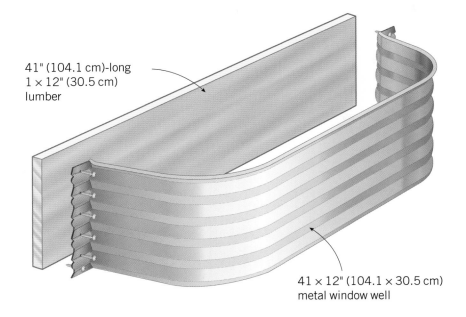

41" (104.1 cm)-long
1 × 12" (30.5 cm)
lumber

41 × 12" (104.1 × 30.5 cm)
metal window well

WINDOW-WELL PLANTING OPTIONS

Though you're not going to plant a prize-winning pumpkin or a bumper crop of zucchini in this smaller raised bed, there are plenty of other options. Mine hold three big pepper plants. Remember, if you're planting peppers and tomatoes, you'll have to stake them, rather than place cages overtop, as the window well isn't quite wide enough to accommodate a tomato cage.

It is deep enough for root veggies, like carrots, turnips, and beets. You could even plant a decent onion harvest. If you placed a trellis behind it, you could plant climbers, like peas, beans, or cucumbers.

Consider planting perennial herbs, like thyme, chives, and oregano. These will come back every year. Or, switch it up with different annuals each year—cilantro, dill, or whatever you use the most!

Drill your screws through the window well into the wood in the dips of the corrugated steel.

This is a very easy project, even for someone who doesn't have woodworking skills. If you don't have a way to cut wood, many lumberyards will size it for you. Then all that is left to do is attach it to the window well, fill it with soil, and plant and water.

PUTTING IT TOGETHER

1. Place the window well on top of the wood and predrill holes in the "low" parts of the corrugated steel.

2. Attach the window well to the wood using the screws.

CHAPTER 5
ECO-FRIENDLY FRONT YARDS

Eco-friendly gardening concepts and their coverage as topics in mainstream media have evolved exponentially over the last few years. Little by little, taking steps to be mindful of the environment when gardening is no longer an outrageous concept only the super environmentally conscious dare to implement. Everyone seems to want to do their part to help, whether it's providing milkweed for monarch butterflies or installing a rain barrel. And every little project counts.

Green roofs, organic veggie gardening, pollinator plants, and xeriscaping are all buzzwords that have been covered in lifestyle and news publications, and it's so nice to see even novice gardeners eager to apply eco-friendly ideas and alternatives to their garden plans. These are not merely fleeting trends; they're concepts that are here to stay.

Whether one owns a home or rents it, that property, whatever the measurements, can be landscaped and planted in a way that supports beneficial insects and wildlife, that doesn't use pesticides or herbicides, and that doesn't require a lot of water to

survive—but that still looks nice from the street. It might not be that traditional look of lawn and foundation planting, but our vision of what a front yard should look like is also evolving (many gardeners have already embraced this).

Speaking of water, these days, gardeners must contend with two extremes: droughts and deluges. And so, besides the planting strategies of creating a haven and food source for beneficial insects, pollinators, and wildlife, rainwater (or the lack of it) is a big issue that many homeowners and renters need to address.

Extreme downpours have become commonplace, resulting in flooded basements, roadways, and yards. Paving paradise has its consequences. Municipalities are catching on to the challenges created by impermeable surfaces and working to implementing solutions such as rain gardens on hell strips and bioswales. Permeable paving, discussed in the next chapter, is another sustainable option to consider when creating pathways and even overhauling a driveway.

Credit: (both) Donna Griffith

Another key factor that anyone who gardens craves is low maintenance. Once established, eco-friendly gardens can reduce the required general maintenance.

Although the ideas and projects in preceding chapters have an inherently eco-conscious bent, this chapter addresses some practical solutions that might be necessary on the property, like the aforementioned rainwater issues or drought-like conditions. Believe it or not, there are some great plants that will thrive in both extremes, so there are some planting ideas and recommendations, too, as well as inspiration to support wildlife and pollinators.

I'm really excited about the pollinator palace I built for my front yard garden, inspired by a design I spotted at the Chelsea Flower Show a couple years ago. It certainly piqued the neighbors' interest. My husband and I had a few people stop on foot or in their cars to ask what it was.

And just as an aside, "wildlife" isn't about supporting those critters that can wreak havoc on a garden—i.e., deer and squirrels (though I mean them no harm)—but rather the wildlife a gardener doesn't mind attracting, like toads, birds, and bats.

Credit: Janet Ennamorato

DEALING WITH RAIN

O ver the last few years, many municipalities have implemented various programs to deal with the environmental impact of heavy rains. For example, there are downspout disconnection programs in place in many areas to divert rainwater from the sewer system (where it used to go) into the yard— away from the house and foundation, of course. This helps prevent sewers from overflowing and flooding surrounding areas in a storm.

Other creative solutions are becoming more widespread. Hell strips and boulevards are being put to use and turned into rain gardens to strategically capture and filter rainwater. Permeable paving solutions are being installed as pathways and driveways so the water has somewhere to go, rather than pooling. And swales are diverting water away from problem areas.

On a smaller scale, rain barrels are often encouraged to capture rainwater. They're a great item to have in the yard, as that basin of conserved water can be used to water gardens and container plants when there is no rain in the forecast. French drains are another way to divert smaller amounts of surface water.

A dry bed works with the slope of the property to carry water away from the house. Credit: Donna Griffith

Water is diverted from the downspout into a rain garden, which will divert the water away from the house, while helping hydrate the plants that surround it. Credit: Donna Griffith

WHY SWALES ARE SWELL

A landscaper who comes to a property to fix a rainwater issue will try to work with the existing lay of the land when drawing up a design. In terms of grading, the trick is getting the water to collect where you want it to go, so working with the shape and slope of the yard is necessary. If water is sitting away from a foundation, generally a dish shape will be created where water can be housed and collected. This is commonly referred to as a swale, or bioswale.

Mike Prong, a certified fusion landscape professional, provides a great analogy to explain how a bioswale works. He equates creating a swale to being a kid at the beach digging a pool and then creating a channel in the sand to divert it, but on a much larger scale. That channel is filled with river rock, which looks nice and is also a functional feature of the garden. You might also see this swath of rock referred to simply as a river rock bed.

A benefit of rain gardening is you can see where the water is moving, as opposed to drainpipes that may have been created underground, making it hard to solve a problem when the system breaks down. The maintenance of a rain garden, on the other hand, is minimal to none—once the initial work is done, there is little ongoing maintenance.

The best first step for a homeowner interested in a rain garden is to consult a professional. Then, they can decide if they want to DIY or hire someone to do the work for them.

In this front yard, the homeowner had water pooling along the front of her house and the entire yard was raised a bit from the sidewalk. Water was sitting too close to the foundation in one spot and running onto the sidewalk in the other. A river rock swale was incorporated into the landscape design to direct the water. The client was also keen to include native and pollinator plants to increase and encourage biodiversity on the property.
Credit: Mike Prong

A rain garden works with the slope of the property to capture rainwater and filter some of it through the ground as it moves off the property.
Credit: Donna Griffith

DOUBLE-DUTY PLANTS

Planting is an important part of the design as the site will require plants that can tolerate a lot of water, as well as drought (the swale provides an irrigation source in between these two extremes). Fernridge Landscaping has shared the plants they most commonly use. These can withstand both excessive rain and drought in a landscape.

SHRUBS

Hydrangea paniculata
'Pee Wee';
Pee Wee Hydrangea

Ilex verticillata
'Berry Poppins';
Berry Poppins Winterberry

Ilex verticillata
'Mr. Poppins';
Mr. Poppins
Winterberry (male)

PERENNIALS

Aster novae-angliae
'Purple Dome';
Purple Dome Aster

Calamintha nepeta
Lesser Calamint

Delphinium elatum
'Blue Lace';
Blue Lace Larkspur

Delphinium elatum
'Pagan Purples';
Pagan Purples larkspur

Digitalis purpurea
'Candy Mountain';
Candy Mountain Foxglove

Echinacea purpurea
'PowWow Wild Berry';
PowWow Wild Berry
Coneflower

Geranium x 'Rozanne'
Azure Rush; Cranesbill

Paeonia
'Pink Parfait';
Pink Parfait Peony

Phlox paniculata
'Bright Eyes';
Bright Eyes Garden Phlox

GRASS

*Pennisetum
alopecuroides*
'Hameln';
Hameln Dwarf Fountain

Top: *Hydrangea paniculata*, middle: *Phlox paniculata*, bottom: *Delphinium elatum*.
Credit: Shutterstock

CAPTURING AND FILTERING RAINWATER

Horticulturist Spencer Hauck of Sandhill Botanicals got rid of his lawn because it was a water hog and was more work than it was worth. The gravel is 18" (45.7 cm) deep and was designed to trap water from the backwash from the pool and downspouts. The grade of the property has the water flowing to the sidewalk, so it does not become trapped in the gravel bed and slowly saturates the ground all around the gardens. The plant material in this garden was chosen based on its interesting appearance and its low-maintenance needs (watering, insect and disease resistance, etc.). This particular region has a strict water ban every summer, starting in June, so the homeowner took that into consideration when planning this garden. Credit: Spencer Hauck

FUSION GARDENING

In the surrounding area where I live, the name Fusion Gardening has been coined—and trademarked!—to describe the practice of blending eco-friendly gardening practices, that work with your landscape and your property's conditions, with traditional garden concepts (i.e., formal versus cottage-garden style).

This concept addresses wet areas of the property, diverting water away from the house and problem areas, as well as increasing biodiversity. There is even a certification program for landscape professionals who want to build fusion gardens for clients.

Fusion gardening isn't a specific style of gardening, it's a concept that works with the design aesthetic you'd like to achieve.

Plant material is carefully chosen (to attract pollinators, filter rainwater, etc.), hardscaping is permeable, allowing rain to soak into the ground, and rainwater from eaves can be artfully diverted in creative ways, from rain chains and rain barrels to rain swales. And an added bonus that all green thumbs can appreciate, is that once they establish themselves, fusion gardens require less maintenance.

A rain garden in action, filtering rainwater during a storm. Credit: Elizabeth Wren

The rain garden on a dry day. The homeowner has a sign from the municipality showing neighbors how the garden works. Credit: Mike Prong

A rain chain can be installed in place of a downspout—you just need to make sure the water has a place to go when it gets to the bottom. Credit: Shutterstom

A clever downspout system in a show garden at Canada Blooms leads water to a sub-irrigated planter. Credit: Tara Nolan

Rain is diverted into this sub-irrigated planter raised bed to water the vegetables from underneath. Credit: Tara Nolan

TIPS FOR CAPTURING RAINWATER ON A BOULEVARD/HELL STRIP

Depending on where you live, there might be a boulevard or hell strip between the sidewalk at the edge of your front yard and the street. In most places, it's owned by the municipality (with the accompanying local bylaws), but homeowners often are tasked with maintenance. Because of their location, boulevards are mainly planted with grass, maybe with a tree plunked in the middle, but always on the front line of salt spray (if you have a winter climate) and car exhaust and people and dogs. Boulevards can also be functional, capturing rainwater and filtering it before it goes into the storm sewer.

If you are going to garden this area, the first step would be to amend the soil. Knowing the conditions this area is subjected to, the second step is choosing hardy plants that will survive. Enthusiastic gardeners also need to be mindful that utilities are often routed under a boulevard, so know that, whatever you do, it isn't necessarily going to be permanent. It's wise to avoid hardscaping or adding some type of accessory, like a giant rock. It's a good idea to find out what lies beneath the area. You'll want to keep your plantings shallow.

Keep in mind the importance of sight lines for cars backing in and out of driveways on either side. Keep all planting material below 29" (73.7 cm).

When figuring out what to plant, parking lots are great indicators of what might work well in these inhospitable areas, which often have poor, unmaintained soil. Plants like shore juniper and spirea may be good options.

At the garden center, keep an eye out for native, salt-tolerant plants. Their crowns are often planted deeper in the soil so they're not afflicted as much by surface pollution.

Hint: Any plant name with a maritime word in the title, like Sea Thrift and Seal Kale, is often a good indication that it will tolerate salt. Sometimes, it's simply a matter of experimenting to find what works.

A stretch of hell strip planted with native wildflower perennials.
Credit: Alamy Stock Photo

Landscape designer Sean James opts for a mix of textures, planting woolly and blue-leaf plants. Plantings include *Veronicastrum* 'Fascination', milkweed, thyme, Invincibelle Spirit smooth hydrangea (described as "bulletproof" in terms of hardiness), fountain grass, globe thistle (beloved by pollinators, but Sean warns it can spread), sea kale, and roses. Credit: Sean James

This boulevard is bermed up so it catches the rainwater as it comes toward it before draining into the storm sewer. Credit: Sean James

THE BENEFITS OF RAIN BARRELS

My neighbor swears her plants are happier when they're watered with rainwater collected in her rain barrel. Rain barrels are typically connected to downspouts from a home's eaves to catch and reserve rainwater that would otherwise spill out into the yard or onto the street and, ultimately, into the storm sewer.

Capturing rainwater to reuse in your garden or yard conserves water resources, as well as saves money on your water bill. According to the World Wildlife Fund, the average roof sheds about 600 gallons (2,271 L) of water for every inch (2.5 cm) of rain. And the United States Environmental Protection Agency states that a rain barrel can save about 1,300 gallons (4,921 L) of water over the peak summer months.

Many municipalities now have "rain barrel days" in spring when homeowners can purchase, or even make their own, rain barrels to install in their yards. And, depending on where you live, there may be a mandate to disconnect downspouts from going directly into the sewer, which used to occur in some areas. Often, the driveway presents a nice, flat area where, if you have the space, you can nestle a rain barrel against the house.

All it takes to get set up with a rain barrel is a downspout connection kit that will send the water into your rain barrel. Some folks even connect and link another rain barrel or two to capture as much rainwater as possible. Rain barrels have a spigot at the bottom to which you can attach a hose (if it doesn't come with one), allowing you to easily fill watering cans with rainwater to hydrate your ornamental and veggie gardens.

Rain barrel kits range in price. There are some fancy ones on the market that allow you to plant a garden in the top. However, creative folks can DIY their own rain barrel at a fraction of the cost. All you need is a 55-gallon (208 L) drum and a few connector parts.

BEFORE YOU ACQUIRE A RAIN BARREL

It's important to note that the collection of rainwater may be restricted, or illegal, in some areas—especially those experiencing drought conditions. Check with your municipality if you are unsure of what is allowed in your area.

Many municipalities now have rain barrel days where homeowners can purchase a pre-fab rain barrel at a good price. Credit: Shutterstock

INSTALLING A RAIN BARREL

DESIGNED FROM *STEP-BY-STEP PROJECTS FOR SELF-SUFFICIENCY*

Cut the downspout to length and reattach the elbow fitting. Add an extension, if necessary.

TOOLS

Drill/driver

Screwdriver

Hacksaw

MATERIALS

Rain barrel

Base material (flagstone)

Downspout hose and fittings

Sheet metal screws

Downspout adapter and extension

Teflon tape

Eye and ear protection

Work gloves

Y ou've brought your shiny new rain barrel home. Now what? The first thing you should do is make sure it has a level place to sit. This may be in your front or side yard or on your driveway. If the area is part of the garden, a square piece of flagstone makes a great base (use a stack if you'd like your rain barrel set higher for easier access). Just be sure to level it. There are also stands available, but be sure they can withstand the weight of your size of barrel (a full rain barrel weighs over 400 pounds [181 kg]). You also need to make sure the overflow water has an outlet directed away from the house. This can be done with a diverter.

These steps assume your rain barrel kit has a spigot installed. If you need to install a spigot, take a look at the DIY rain barrel steps on pages 161 to 163.

1. Connect the overflow tube, ensuring it is pointed away from the foundation of your home.

2. Using a hacksaw, cut the downspout to the appropriate length that allows the barrel to fit underneath it. Reconnect the elbow fitting to the downspout using sheet metal screws.

3. If necessary, attach a length of flexible downspout extension to the elbow, which will lead water into the rain barrel.

4. Instead of cutting off your downspout, you can install a diverter kit to direct water into the rain barrel. Most kits have a feature that directs water runoff to the original downspout if the rain barrel is full.

If your barrel comes with a downspout adapter, cut away a segment of the downspout to install it, which will divert water into the barrel.

MAKE YOUR OWN RAIN BARREL OUT OF A TRASH CAN

PROJECT FROM *STEP-BY-STEP PROJECTS FOR SELF-SUFFICIENCY*

TOOLS

Pencil or marker

Drill with spade bit

Jigsaw

Hole saw

Channel-type pliers

MATERIALS

32- to 44-gallon (121 to 166.5 l) plastic trash can

Barb fitting with nut for overflow hose

1½" (3.8 cm) sump drain hose for overflow ¾" (1.9 cm) hose bibb or sillcock (brass or PVC)

¾" (1.9 cm) male pipe coupling ¾" (1.9 cm) bushing or bulkhead connector

Teflon tape Silicone caulk Fiberglass window screening Cargo strap with ratchet or bungee cord

A large plastic trash can is perfect for converting into a rain barrel. Choose a heavy-duty plastic variety with a snap-on lid (if you have one kicking around that you aren't using, even better). Most standard trash cans hold about 32 gallons (121 L). But if you happen across one that holds 44 gallons (166.5 L), you'll be able to capture more water. A used barrel or a large plastic food-service barrel could also do the trick. If you are upcycling, make sure the vessel wasn't used for dangerous chemicals or other substances in its previous life. You don't want to spread that onto your plants, especially edibles, and you don't want it around pets or people, either.

The window screening recommended in the materials list is to cover the hole where the water flows in to prevent debris from getting into your rain barrel, as well as preventing mosquitoes from laying eggs in the standing water.

PUTTING IT TOGETHER

1. Mark the size and shape of your opening in the top of the barrel (this is where the water will pour in from the eave)—if you are using a food barrel, mark a large semicircle on the top. If you're using a plastic garbage can with a lid, mark a 12" (30.5 cm)-diameter circle in the center of the lid. Drill a starter hole and then use the jigsaw to cut out the intended space for opening.

2. Drill a hole near the top of the barrel for the overflow fitting. Thread the barb fitting into the hole and secure it to the barrel on the inside with the retainer nut and rubber washer (if provided). Slide the overflow hose onto the barbed end of the elbow until the end of the hose seats against the elbow flange.

3. Drill the access hole for the spigot (either a hose bibb or sillcock). Tighten the stem of the sillcock onto a threaded coupling inserted into the access hole. Inside the barrel, slip a rubber washer onto the coupling end and then tighten a threaded bushing over the coupling to create a seal. Apply a strip of Teflon tape to all the threaded parts before making each connection. Caulk around the spigot with clear silicone caulk.

4. Measure a piece of fiberglass screening so it fits over the top of the garbage can and secure it around the rim using a cargo strap or bungee cord so it's stretched tightly. Snap the lid over the top. The way this is put together makes for easy cleaning of the mesh and bin. It's also easy to empty for winter (see sidebar, opposite).

Drill an access hole to install the spigot and coupling assembly in the bottom of the trash can.

Secure fiberglass screening around the top of the barrel to filter out impurities and prevent insets from getting into the water.

RAIN BARREL MAINTENANCE

To prevent your rain barrel from cracking, it's important to drain it completely at the end of fall. If possible, turn it upside-down to store. Make sure the spigot is set to open. Use a diverter to make sure any rainwater or snowmelt from your downspout does not collect in the rain barrel during winter.

During summer, make sure that leaves and debris aren't able to get into the rain barrel, which could clog the hose. If there is an open hole at the top, it's a good idea to add a piece of netting to prevent mosquitoes from laying eggs in the standing water.

In spring, check the barrel and hoses thoroughly for any cracks and take a good look inside (if possible) before setting it up for the season.

Keep the water supply in your rain barrel fresh by draining it regularly. Before winter in cold climates, drain the barrel and store it upside-down so water inside does not freeze and crack the barrel.

GARDENING FOR INSECTS AND WILDLIFE

As habitat diminishes, our own front yards (and backyards, too!) can be used to provide critical shelter and food sources for beneficial insects, animals, reptiles, birds, and amphibians. Many of the ideas collected in this book naturally help support these goals, namely to attract valuable pollinators and beneficial insects to the garden through strategic planting. However, another critical element is to provide nesting and shelter sites, as well as water.

Sometimes, messages to gardeners can be confusing. Where I live, West Nile virus is a problem, so homeowners are told not to have standing water on their properties, so as to prevent mosquitoes from breeding. On the other hand, gardeners are encouraged to have bird baths and shallow vessels for bees to drink from.

I suppose you have to choose what is best for you and your family. All I can recommend is trying to create a balanced eco-system you feel comfortable with.

PLANTING AND PLANNING TO RECEIVE SPECIAL CERTIFICATIONS

A number of organizations now provide guidance and special habitat designations, encouraging home gardeners to do their part. It can be overwhelming thinking of all the things you might want to do to help support wildlife and beneficial insects in your garden. We read about planting milkweed for monarchs, leaving water sources for bees, and sowing meadows for pollinators. Start with one thing and move on to another the following year.

Some organizations take this dedication to conservation a step further with certificates and signs you can hang in the garden. Here are a few that might be of interest:

THE NATIONAL WILDLIFE FEDERATION

The National Wildlife Federation (nwf.org) provides a handy checklist that can then be used to apply for a Certified Wildlife Habitat designation. The checklist indicates what a homeowner should provide in terms of food, water, cover, and places to raise young, as well as documenting your sustainable practices. "Every habitat garden is a step toward replenishing resources for wildlife such as bees, butterflies, birds, and amphibians—both locally and along migratory corridors," the site says. Upon qualifying, you can get a Certified Wildlife Habitat sign to hang in your garden.

THE CANADIAN WILDLIFE FEDERATION

Certifying your garden as a wildlife-friendly habitat can happen by filling out an application form where you check all the boxes that apply to what you're doing in the garden. There is also an option to include a sketch of your garden. Necessary elements include one or more sources of water, food, and shelter in the garden and to vouch that you use earth-friendly gardening practices to maintain it. If you meet the criteria, you will receive a certificate and decal to display.

THE MILLION POLLINATOR GARDEN MOVEMENT

The original initiative, The Million Pollinator Garden Challenge, surpassed its goal to register a million gardens and landscapes to support pollinators, but is still going strong. People are encouraged to plant gardens for bees, butterflies, birds, bats, and other pollinators. It was dubbed a nationwide (United States) call to action, but it's amazing to look at the map to see all the different countries around the world where people have registered.

IN THE ZONE

Where I live falls into the Carolinian zone, what's been dubbed a biodiverse eco-region between the Great Lakes. WWF-Canada and an organization called Carolinian Canada have created a program called In the Zone to encourage home gardeners to support native wildlife by providing food and shelter. A checklist narrows each to-do toward creating a climate-smart garden.

Think of supporting beneficial insects, animals, reptiles, birds, and amphibians when selecting plants for your garden.
Credit: Tara Nolan

Red polka dots were painted on this home to attract hummingbirds to the neighborhood—and it worked.
Credit: Tara Nolan

USING A HOUSE AND FRONT YARD GARDEN TO ATTRACT HUMMINGBIRDS

When chef and musician Chuck Currie was trying to attract hummingbirds to his East Vancouver yard, he planted bushes and flowers that would attract them, but it didn't seem to work. His girlfriend worked at a retailer called Wild Birds Unlimited, which kept a large map of Vancouver with hummingbird sightings. On the map, all the hummingbirds were in the west end of the city where all the flower gardens are. There were none on Chuck's side of the city, where everyone has vegetable gardens.

After cleverly painting red polka dots on his house (the color signals to hummingbirds that nectar is nearby), there were soon multiple pins showing up in East Vancouver—all of them at Chuck's address.

The garden itself got a little wild—Currie dubbed it "the jungle," and says his main gardening tool was a machete to cut back the extremely aggressive blackberries. The berry bush was so unruly, their mailperson threatened to stop bringing the mail because the thorns were so large and profuse!

Eventually, Chuck decided to start over with the garden. A couple of small bulldozers took out the existing garden. He added new soil and created, what he describes as, a more cultivated garden.

Not only are hummingbirds attracted to the yard, other birds, such as American bushtits and goldfinches, enjoy the yard, too.

ASSEMBLE A POLLINATOR PALACE

DESIGNED BY JOHN CULLEN OF JOHN CULLEN GARDENS LTD.
BUILT BY TARA NOLAN
PHOTOS BY DONNA GRIFFITH

TOOLS

Power miter saw in case you want to cut "levels" from wood

Eye protection

MATERIALS

Metal gabions or old metal milk crates

Plywood or metal sheets cut to fit the length and width of the gabion

Yard debris, such as sticks, pine cones, moss, dried flowers, etc.

Mason bee nesting tubes

Insect hotels have become pretty ubiquitous in public gardens, garden centers, and nurseries, as well as the gardens of green thumbs everywhere. There are lots of DIYs to be found and astute manufacturers have zoned in on the trend. The purpose of these structures is to provide nesting sites and lodging for solitary bees and wasps, lacewings, beetles, and other beneficial insects.

At the 2017 RHS Chelsea Flower Show in London, England, there were some pretty stunning insect hotels on display in the gardens. But in the Great Pavilion, I encountered a very unique structure for pollinators, artistically assembled, though a little wilder looking: the pollinator palace. Conceived by John Cullen of John Cullen Gardens, gabions filled with layers of live plant material and items found in nature were placed among a regular garden with trees, flowers, and groundcover.

"Inspiration for the Pollinator Palaces came firstly from a sustainability point of view," says John. "I wanted something that would last forever—often the wooden bug hotels start to rot down and, in time, just become homes for bugs and not pollinators." John was also keen to find something that gave an initial tidy look. "We are often met with the misconception that if you garden for wildlife, it needs to be messy," he explains. "The steel gabions throw all of this out the window." Rather than a messy piles of logs or twigs in the corner of the garden, John explains that you can now have a tidy pile that can look like art.

Metal gabions with shelves are used to create a layering effect in John Cullen's pollinator palaces exhibited at the RHS Chelsea Flower Show. Credit: Tara Nolan

John's concept is fluid enough that you can decide which pollinators you would like to attract:

- Solitary bees are always on the lookout for a safe quiet place to nest. Using cardboard tubes within your palace creates spaces for them to make nests for their larvae.

- Moths and butterflies love places to cool down.

- You can also create a feeding station on the top of the palace by placing a large plate with fruit for butterflies to feed on.

Every palace that John Cullen's company creates is unique and tailored for the client. I decided to create my own to display in my front garden and set out to source a decorative gabion. At one point, I was only able to find wholesalers that sold gabions. But on my failed trip to find a salad table for my lettuce side table project (see page 126), I found these delightfully rusty old milk crates. Three of them, when stacked, make the perfect makeshift "gabion." I couldn't wait to get them home.

Because it was spring and I don't do an extensive fall cleanup, I was able to gather some debris, like small branches, and I scored hydrangea sticks from a neighbor. I also gathered moss that covers some old patio stones at the back of my property, carefully scraping it off with my soil knife. Pine cones were collected and delivered by a friend. And I ordered the nesting tubes for Mason bees online.

John Cullen says he uses hydrangea heads to create shelter spots for bees and ladybirds, rather than actual homes. He also says that once any plant material breaks down, it can be replaced yearly or with the seasons.

My finished project is nestled among a perennial garden near the street. The garden is planted with a plethora of pollinator-friendly plants, like catmint, lavender, echinacea, milkweed, ninebark, liatris, and more, so there are a lot of pollinators that frequent the garden.

I did attach the three milk crates to each other using zip ties, just in case anyone decides they want my pollinator palace to grace their own yard. Layers can easily be swapped out over time, but I'll have to add new zip ties.

PUTTING IT TOGETHER

You can customize your layers however you like or with whatever materials you have close at hand. Here is my layering order:

In the bottom milk crate, I placed layers of moss, followed by hydrangea sticks. The great thing about the milk crates as opposed to a gabion is there is a natural shelf added when stacked.

I placed the second crate on top and layered it with bark, twigs, and meatier sticks gathered from my yard. Then, I cut a square of plywood slightly smaller than the square shape of the milk crate and sat it on top of the stick layer.

John Cullen uses metal shelves cut to size to support each floor for his pollinator palaces created in gabions.

This was the only layer where I needed a shelf because everything else was easy to stack, plus I had the natural shelves created by the crates' bottoms.

On this "platform," I stacked the Mason bee nesting tubes before adding the third crate. In this last crate, I added the pine cones, another layer of sticks and twigs, and some moss on top. At the back of the crate, I nestled a little terracotta pot with alyssum, which attracts parasitic wasps, beneficial insects that take care of some bad guys.

I used branches and twigs found around my yard to create a couple layers in my pollinator palace.

The bottom of each milk crate featured a nature shelf, meaning I didn't need to cut too much wood to separate the layers. The solitary nesting tubes for Mason bees are resting on a square piece of plywood cut to size.

I found my Mason bee nesting tubes online and was delighted to find some filled in during the summer.

Credit: Tara Nolan

SOLITARY NESTING TUBES

John Cullen recommends using the cardboard tubes, which I was able to source online. "If bamboo or other wooden tubes are used, you have to ensure that the insides are baby smooth," he explains. "Any splinters, even tiny ones, can spear the emerging young in spring. We source all the tubes from a company in the United Kingdom that specialize in solitary bees."

CHAPTER 6
FRONT YARD GARDEN EMBELLISHMENTS

Although planting and growing are the fun parts for gardeners, there are certain elements, some of them absolutely essential, that make up various structural elements of a front yard garden. A lot of these generally fall under the umbrella of "hardscaping."

Practical hardscaping components include driveways, paths, and walkways, edging that separates garden from grass, fences (picket and privacy), and garden walls (low or high). Hedges and trees also fall under the structural side of things, even though they're living components of the garden.

One or all of these aspects can be incorporated into your front yard design and the style you choose will be integral to the overall look that you're hoping to achieve. Depending on the scale of your project, your project will either be doable in a few days, something to chip away at throughout the season, or a complete overhaul that requires you to call in a professional (or two) to handle the labor.

Creating a more eco-friendly driveway, for example, is a giant project unto itself. Driveway materials aren't replaced very often. It's more of a one-time project you hope will last. And it can certainly be a long-term front yard goal that can be shelved until you're ready to start researching what you'd like to replace the asphalt with. There are some great sustainable, more eco-friendly options now that homeowners are turning to for greener spaces. And many companies are upgrading their product lines accordingly to include such offerings, like permeable paving solutions for paths, patios, and driveways.

Smaller projects, such as pathways or digging in a privacy hedge, can become weekend projects on your to-do list, filling in the blanks of your garden vision. Speaking of vision, event these smaller utilitarian elements are just as vital to a front yard garden as the plants, contributing to the look and feel of your garden design.

If you are consulting with a landscape professional, ask them how you can maintain the flow of a front yard garden, extending it into the side yard and planting or hardscaping according to the conditions, if space allows. From a design standpoint, if you're looking at each outdoor space as a series of rooms, side yards are basically hallways to the backyard, but they can be extra rooms, too, depending on the square footage.

There are endless options for hardscaping and other projects, but I've zeroed in on a few ideas that fall on the less-labor-intensive side of things. I've seen really gorgeous photos of high-contrast, low-growing groundcover plants that cover driveways, which inspired me to take sedum mats, which are used more often in greenhouse applications, to fill a width of front yard that, technically, a car or truck could park over or on either side of. My mowing border morphed into a full-on garden path, but it allowed me to display both ideas as construction progressed.

I've also touched a bit on side yards. These spaces may blend into the front yard, or you can establish a clear delineation between the front, side, and backyard. What's interesting about side yards is they share a property line with a neighbor, so often there are interesting features, like gates and privacy fences involved, not to mention other options that could factor in to bigger decisions to be made. If you live on a corner lot, the side yard can be every bit as on display as the front, requiring its own exclusive design. I still think a picket fence is a great way to provide a bit of distance and privacy between the property and sidewalk or street. Hedges work well, too, especially if you're seeking a bit more privacy.

Side yard conditions usually present unique challenges, from complete shade and poor soil, to drainage issues. If the conditions are right, you may be lucky enough to extend your plantings along the side yard. Narrow raised beds, like the window well creation, can make up for poor soil, while allowing space for some food crops, if needed.

This chapter presents a series of (mostly) building projects to enhance your front yard, driveway, and side yard.

A wrought iron fence allows passerby to admire the garden—from the other side.
Credit: Donna Griffith

PLANT A SEDUM CARPET

DESIGNED AND INSTALLED BY TARA NOLAN
PHOTOS BY DONNA GRIFFITH
SEDUM MATS PROVIDED BY SEDUM MASTER

TOOLS	MATERIALS
Wheelbarrow (for moving the sedum mats)	Sedum mats to fit the intended garden space
Rake	Soil (look for a blend formulated for growing sedum)
Shovel	
Soil knife	

As some gardeners work to turn their lawns into garden, others have transformed their driveways into a garden—but one in which cars can still park. This is a novel idea, but it's one that adds a whole new level of visual appeal in place of ordinary asphalt or a concrete driveway.

Groundcover plants need to be chosen according to a low maximum height. I've seen moss, creeping thyme, different varieties of sedum, and more used to fill a driveway garden—which is why, when I approached friends about turning a small strip of their front yard into a driveway garden, the first thing I thought about using was sedum mats.

With parking at a premium on a one-way street, this urban semidetached house has the space for two cars between the house and the sidewalk. As such, there is no front lawn. Most of the driveway is asphalt, but there was a small section of (removable) patio stones. The perfect place for a carpet of colorful sedum. And the placement was such that a second car could fit nicely overtop, with the driveway garden fitting well within the wheels of a car.

I first encountered sedum mats as a suggested option for green roof plans. Sedums are drought and heat tolerant, provide winter interest, and can survive in poorer soil. Another bonus? Sedums attract butterflies, bumblebees, and hummingbirds. They are also lower maintenance than a lawn in the long run. Why not use them on a driveway?

Some sedum mats are rolled up like sod, but mine came in tiles because of the smaller space I was covering. They were very easy to install and the finished result looked like one long continuous, interesting, multi-colored carpet. Some of the sedums had even started to bloom, so this little island of vegetation was ready to attract pollinators. Furthermore, it looks so gorgeous, the homeowners are now loathe to allow a visiting car to use the spot.

Minimum sun exposure is three to four hours per day. Also noting that it is a bit of a walkway, sedum mats will suffer through the odd step, but are not meant for constant treading.

I was just filling a small space, but I recommend, if you're tearing up an entire driveway, that you consult a professional to help assess grade and runoff management.

INSTALLING A SEDUM MAT CARPET

Sedum mats need 3 to 4" (7.6 to 10.2 cm) of growing space beneath them. It was recommended that I create a base of 3 to 4" (7.6 to 10.2 cm) of green-roof growing medium, which is a special blend that allows for drainage. Because there was grit beneath the patio stones, I added regular garden soil overtop instead, as recommended by a local nursery that happens to sell the sedum mats. Use a rake to spread the soil evenly throughout the entire area.

----

1. Lay out each sedum mat "tile" so it fits snug against either the sides of whatever your border is or the mat beside it.

----

2. Use the soil knife to trim any pieces that don't fit into the space. Turn the tile so the outer edge isn't the trimmed one. The inner trimmed edge will fit seamlessly against the other tile, whereas the outer edge will retain that wild, natural look that spills over the edges a bit.

----

3. Give your sedum mats a good daily watering until the plants become established.

Sedum mats stack easily in the car—they just need a little fluff when they get to their destination. Also, be sure not to store them stacked! Credit: Tara Nolan

Sedum mat "tiles" are laid out like pieces of carpet. Fifteen whole mats were used to fill a 3 × 11' (0.9 × 3.4 m) area.

Use a rake to evenly spread the soil throughout the garden space that's been exposed.

I found using my A.M. Leonard Soil Knife to be the easiest way to slice through the mats that needed to be trimmed to fit the space.

Sedum mats from Sedum Master can feature over a dozen species, including Acre, Acre 'Oktoberfest', Album, *ellacombianum, floriferum, forster; lanum*, 'Silver Stone', *glaucophyllum, hispanicum, hybridum,* 'Czar's Gold', *kamtschaticum, reflexum, selskianum,* 'Goldilocks', *sexangulare, spurium, coccinneum, spurium,* 'Summer Glory' and 'Voodoo', and *stenopetalum.*

USING PERMEABLE PAVERS FOR DRIVEWAYS AND PATHWAYS

My niece's school recently "unpaved" part of the schoolyard, laying mulch and building gardens in its place. What if people started unpaving their driveways and pathways (when they're at the crossroads of needing to be replaced), instead of spreading buckets of blacktop over the asphalt every so often to give them a fresh, shiny appearance?

Urban flooding in the past few years has reinforced that water will always demand a place to go. As traditional asphalt and concrete don't absorb water, it either pools in low spots or is washed into the sewer system, collecting pollutants along the way. Depending on the rain event, excessive water can overwhelm storm drains and sewers, lakes, and rivers, leading to homes and businesses being flooded. Furthermore, that water drags pollutants along with it, instead of simply soaking into the ground.

Driveway design has come a long way, especially because the thought of tearing up an asphalt driveway is a pretty monumental task. But if the material is on its last legs, why not reimagine it with a more sustainable solution?

Besides just going the straight-up gravel route, there are modern options available that are engineered to deal with and allow for excessive rain to be absorbed into the ground. These materials can be used for both driveways and pathways.

In speaking with landscape designers, it's clear there is a big push in the stone and hardscaping industry for eco-friendly pavers. Even installation methods, like paver placement, is being rethought. Tightly spaced pavers might keep those weeds down, but they don't let any water through.

This homeowner was looking for an eco-friendly solution, both for the driveway and the garden design. This driveway was built using a permeable paving material. The front yard garden has been filled with medicinal, edible, or fermentable plants—most plants have a designated use (included are hosta 'Regal Splendor', juniper, echinacea, *Monarda fistulosa,* and yew). Credit: Mike Prong

In a large-scale situation, excess water pools because pavers are placed so closely together that they don't leave any significant gaps for water to drain through or they impede the water's flow.

Several companies have invented products featuring permeable pavers, within which water can more easily disperse. Homeowners looking for a sustainable upgrade to their traditional driveway will discover permeable pavers that allow water to drain through them, based on spacers that create bigger gaps than what has been used in the past.

Some of these sustainable products come as grids that are filled with gravel or that can be planted with grass, whereas others fit certain sizes of pavers. All allow water to filter through without creating runoff. And most should be able to withstand harsh winter weather.

An old, deteriorating driveway was removed in order to install an EcoRaster Bloxx permeable paving system. The pavers are made from 100 percent post-consumer waste and recycled rubber. The driveway promotes storm water management with a high filtration rate, preventing runoff. Credit: EcoRaster

THE BENEFITS OF A MOWING BORDER

I didn't realize how useful a mowing border would be until I decided to plant a swath of bulbs along the edge of my front garden that abuts the lawn. Once the grass started to grow in the spring and the bulbs came up, it was really hard to mow and use the whippersnapper without nicking the tulips and muscari and other interesting varieties that I'd planted.

And, so, it was decided that a mowing border would be installed to create some space between the lawn and the perennial garden.

For this project, simply edge the garden, leaving a trench the width of your patio stones. Dig in each stone, paying attention to the curve of the garden. Backfill along the garden side with soil. It's likely the existing sod will provide the support needed on the lawn side. Use a level to ensure each stone is straight.

A mowing border project can be as complex as pouring cement or as simple as digging in patio stones. These ones were purchased at a discount because they were upcycled from a previous project.
Credit: Donna Griffith

CREATE A CONRETE MOWING BORDER

PROJECT FROM *BLACK + DECKER: THE COMPLETE OUTDOOR BUILDER*

TOOLS

Rope or garden hose

Excavation tools

Mason's string

Hand tamper

Maul

Circular saw

Drill

Concrete mixing tools

Margin trowel

Eye and ear protection

Work gloves

MATERIALS

Wood concrete float

Concrete edger

1 × 1" (2.5 × 2.5 cm) wood stakes

¼" (6 mm) hardboard

1" (2.5 cm) wood screws

Fiber-reinforced concrete

Acrylic concrete sealer

Poured concrete edging is the perfect way to follow the curves of a garden.

Poured concrete creates a smooth mowing border between the grass and garden. This requires creating a form into which you can pour the concrete mix. To blend with the lawn and garden, keep the edging low to the ground, about 1" (2.5 cm) above grade.

PUTTING IT TOGETHER

1. Use a rope or garden hose to form the contours of the edging. If you're creating a straight line, use stakes and mason's string to mark the area. Plan for the edging to be at least 5" (12.7 cm) wide.

2. Dig a trench between the lines you've marked that's about 3" (7.6 cm) wider than you'd like your finished project to be. Dig to a depth that allows for a 4" (10.2 cm)-thick curb that will sit about 1" (2.5 cm) above grade. Use a hand tamper or a piece of landscape timber to compact the soil at the bottom of the trench.

3. Drive a 1 × 1 × 12" (2.5 × 2.5 × 30.5 cm) wood stake every 18" (45.7 cm) along the edges of the trench.

4. Use strips of ¼" (6 mm)-thick hardboard to create the form, including the curves. Attach 4" (10.2 cm)-wide strips to the insides of the stakes using 1" (2.5 cm) wood screws.

5. Cut spacers from 1 × 1" (2.5 × 2.5 cm) stock to fit snugly inside the form, placed every 3' (0.9 m) or so. This will maintain the same width the length of the project.

6. Mix the concrete to a firm, workable consistency and pour it inside the form. Use your margin trowel to spread it evenly along the form.

7. Once the bleed water disappears, smooth the surface of your edging using a wood float. With the margin trowel, cut 1" (2.5 cm)-deep control joints across the width of the curb every 3' (0.9 m). Tool the side edges of the curb with an edger. Allow the concrete to cure and seal it according to the package directions. Remove the form after 3 days.

Stake along the edges of the trench, every 18" (45.7 cm) using 1 × 1 × 12" (2.5 × 2.5 × 30.5 cm) wood stakes.

Add spacers inside the form to maintain a consistent width.

Once the bleed water disappears, smooth the surface with a wood float.

OTHER MOWING BORDER IDEAS

Here are some other border project styles you might want to consider.

Using plastic edging to define the border between a garden and a lawn is an efficient way to prevent grass from creeping into the garden. Credit: Shutterstock

Use old bricks or pavers to define a garden area. Credit: Shutterstock

Edging the garden itself with an edging tool creates a very clean line, but it requires maintenance. Credit: Shutterstock

BUILD A GARDEN PATH

PROJECT DESIGNED AND BUILT BY RICH AUGER
PHOTOS BY DONNA GRIFFITH

TOOLS

Measuring tape

Edger

Wheelbarrow

Shovel

Ground tamper

Level

Mallet

MATERIALS

Screening

Landscape edging (optional)

Pea gravel

Patio pavers (to line the path)

Decorative patio stones (for the center)

Garden paths add style and function to a front yard garden. There are so many great options to consider, but, ultimately, it comes down to a design that works with the overall aesthetic of the garden, your home, and your budget.

Functionally, a path moves you somewhere logical—from the front yard to the backyard, to a seating area, to a piece of garden art, to the front door. A path can connect two areas, or garden "rooms." A path can also be a variety of stepping stones that move you around the garden, protecting plants from footsteps and providing little islands from which to weed and plant and water.

Some elements to take into consideration when planning a garden path include choosing materials that don't become slippery when wet and working with the landscape to avoid issues such as water pooling or having to get rid of a tree or digging out plants.

Consider the complexity of the project you choose to undertake. Consider your skills when deciding whether you can DIY or should call in a professional. We relished the DIY challenge, as we had been envisioning a pathway for some time. For this project, based on the slope of our property, my husband and I wanted to create a path that led from the road and connected to the existing concrete path that leads into the backyard. We quickly realized the natural curve of the garden, with its brand-new mowing border, was logically the best place for it. In fact, the mowing border became part of the pathway. My mowing border widened exponentially.

We knew we wanted to use pea gravel and also add stepping areas. We thought about strips of pallet wood, but they would break down over time and were a bit rustic looking when matched with the pea gravel. That led to the thought of using large flat hunks of stone that formed a patio of sorts around an old flagpole at the back of the property. Those stones turned out to be a bit wide. In the meantime, our neighbor was trying to get rid of more stepping stone–sized pavers with a natural look. They were perfect.

I felt good about upcycling two sets of materials for this project. The pavers that line the path are in the same upcycled style used for the mowing border (luckily there were some left!). And our neighbors were happy to find a new home for their stones.

Visually, the project came together really well and I enjoy moseying down the path to water and weed, to snip flowers from the perennial garden for bouquets, or just to see what's in bloom.

THE STEPS TO A GARDEN PATH

String was used to mark the path. A piece of wood cut to the exact width of the path helped with consistency when spacing, especially around curves. Paths are generally about 2 to 3' (0.6 to 0.9 m) wide. You could also use spray paint as a marker, if you wish.

----

1. The next step was to use the edger to systematically cut out the sod. You could use the cardboard trick (see page 24) to break down the grass, but this was a quicker option, even though cutting up sod is no small task! Our sod was thrown into the compost pile as the municipality does not take it in yards bags where I live.

Make sure the depth matches whatever edging you will add to the outside of the path. You don't want it to stick up above the grass or mulch line, creating a tripping hazard.

Some DIYers may consider using landscape fabric as an extra layer underneath the screening to keep the weeds down.

The path ended up following the natural curve of the mowing border that edges the garden. You can see another angle of the live-edge raised bed from page 114 pictured, as well.

A tamper, which can be rented or purchased at a hardware or big box store, is used to flatten the screening for stability.

A scrap piece of 2 × 4" (5.1 × 10.2 cm) and a mallet are used to ensure the edging pavers are uniform.

Use a level to ensure both the edging pavers and the path itself is level (except, of course, on a slope).

2. Add the screening to the carved-out pathway and use the tamper to flatten it down. The hardscaping company helped us figure out how much we needed based on the length of the path and a depth of about 2" (5.1 cm).

We had a load of screening and a load of pea gravel delivered on our driveway at the same time. It was transported to the path in a wheelbarrow.

3. Once the screening is in, set your hose nozzle to a light spray and spray down the screening. This helps it settle and keeps the dust down. (We had a well-timed rainfall that did the job for us!) Tamp down one more time for good measure.

4. Add the patio pavers along the edges, making sure the tops are at even heights. You may want to add metal edging on the outside of the pavers first. This, in theory, will keep the pathway more stable over time.

5. Use the mallet and a piece of lumber to tamp down the pavers so they're level with the grass line. Use a level to make sure they're straight.

6. The next steps can be interchangeable, depending on how you want to finish your pathway. You can add the pea gravel (a least 2" [5.1 cm] deep) to the pathway, carefully raking it out over the screening and then add the stepping stones. Or, you can place the stepping stones where you'd like them and add the pea gravel around them. Either way, ensure that the stepping stones and pea gravel are level with the edging and lawn. You might want to give this level a rinse with the hose, as well.

7. Using your scrap piece of wood and the mallet, go along the entire pathway to make sure all the edging pavers are even.

OTHER PATHWAYS TO PONDER

Here are some other path project styles you might want to consider.

This path leads from the street up to the modern home. Wide paving stones are lined by lavender and the spaces between each one are filled with a larger size of gravel.
Credit: Donna Griffith

The brick path leading up to this home is made from the original bricks of the house. The dinosaur kale creeping toward the path is hard to miss—but it proves that edibles can have ornamental qualities in a front yard garden!
Credit: Donna Griffith

In this garden by Bethesda Garden Design, ornamental grasses line a front walkway laid with unevenly shaped stone for a more natural look.
Credit: Janet Davis

There are lots of great options now for eco-friendly interlocking bricks that look like traditional pavers, but allow water to drain rather than pool.
Credit: Shutterstock

ADDING HEDGES FOR PRIVACY

In a front yard garden, building a high fence from the side of one's house to the street isn't really the neighborly thing to do. However, if you're craving privacy, a hedge seems to be a kinder, less aggressive way of seeking refuge in one's own yard. As part of a garden plan, a hedge can be integrated into the overall landscape, blending in to create a haven for birds and insects.

Hedges are also a great option if you live on a busy street. Although they won't completely block noise, gardeners do use hedges in an attempt to reduce it. And they can, at least, provide a lush barrier behind which you can enjoy your property—however big or small.

Consult your municipality to check how far from the sidewalk, street, or fire hydrant (if one is on your property) your hedge must be planted. Also, are there height restrictions in your area? You should also consult your neighbor as a courtesy if the hedge is being planted between your property and theirs. Lastly, keep your hedge well pruned and be sure to read the growing information on the plant tag to ensure you provide the right growing conditions and care to your plants.

Certain varieties of roses can form a really stunning flowering hedge. Pictured here is Rainbow Knock Out lining a pathway. When planting, place each rose bush 3' (0.9 m) away from the center of the next to promote good air circulation, as well as provide the space it needs to grow. Credit: Star Roses & Plants

PLANTS THAT MAKE GREAT HEDGES

Evergreen hedges will remain green throughout the year, whereas deciduous varieties might have interesting flowers and leaves that will change color throughout the seasons, but then drop before winter. Here are some popular hedge choices:

Arborvitae: Arborvitae is a popular hedge plant because of how dense the foliage is—and it stays green all year long. Varieties include American Arborvitae and Emerald Green Arborvitae.

Weigela: Although their blooms are the star of the show, leaf color can differ among varieties, from the deep burgundy-green of Date Night Tuxedo (with white flowers) to the more variegated cream and green (with pinkish purple flowers) of My Monet Purple Effect.

Forsythia: A forsythia hedge only blooms in spring, but those brilliant yellow blooms are worth the wait! The rest of the year it's a lovely green shrub.

Boxwood: Easy to shape, boxwoods give that nice dense interwoven look to a hedge.

Consider using a flowering shrub as a hedge. Credit: Tara Nolan

A *Cornus mas* (Cornelian cherry dogwood) InstantHedge being planted. This variety has bright yellow flowers in spring, followed by dark red cherries in summer. The plant is easy to shape, has dense foliage, and is esistant to pests and diseases.
Credit: InstantHedge

A HEDGE IN A BOX

Unless you purchase mature shrubs, rather than a small starter pot, a hedge will take a while to grow to form that nice, interlaced, seamless look, not to mention provide adequate height for privacy. A company called InstantHedge has created a quick and easy planting solution in the form of a hedge that comes in a box and is ready to plant upon delivery. Plants are grown in a field in foursomes so, when you receive them, you plant each "strip" in the ground.

You can choose which size of shrub you'd like (3 to 4' [0.9 to 1.2 m] or 4 to 6' [1.2 to 1.8 m]) from more than 25 varieties of evergreen or deciduous hedges. Because they've been grown together, they already have that entwined look of a hedge. All you need to do is dig a trench where you'd like them to go and plant them. If you opt for them to come in a cardboard box for delivery, simply plant the whole thing.

PERGOLAS AND ARBORS

Pergolas and arbors are similar structures and both are generally associated with backyards. Arbors often lead people around the side of a house into a backyard. But a pergola in a front yard is more of a novel idea. It certainly requires space, but when cleverly designed with a home's façade and shape, it can blend well into a front yard garden.

The function of an arbor is, essentially, to lead you from one part of your garden to another. Visually, it acts as a doorway, leading to another area. Depending on the flow of the property, an arbor would be well situated leading from the front yard garden to the side yard or from the back of the side yard into the backyard. Some arbors include a gate. If you set up your garden as a series of rooms, an arbor could also lead you to a more private area of the garden.

I've seen some arbors with benches built into the sides, so an arbor can also serve as a seating area where you could tuck yourself away with a book, hopefully under some shade, on a hot summer day.

Arbors are perfect for training vines or climbing plants. It's common to see vining plants climbing up and winding their tendrils around the structure as they grow, creating a living doorway.

Common plants to train up an arbor include wisteria, clematis, and climbing roses. If you're trying to sneak a few veggies into the garden, a scarlet runner bean would add lots of visual interest. The vibrant red blooms attract hummingbirds and other pollinators to the garden—and then come the beans! Depending on the sides of the structure, cucumbers, cucamelons, and peas could also work.

This garden belongs to a young family who wanted to be in their front yard to experience their kids and neighborhood kids playing, as they tend to play in the front yards. They grow their own vegetables and so incorporated the front yard as vegetable, herb, and landscaped gardens because that is where they get most of the sun on the property.
Credit: Donna Griffith

HOW TO TRAIN A VINE UP A PERGOLA, TRELLIS, OR ARCHWAY

When choosing vining plants, first do a little research to see which plants will suit the structure you have. When you get the vining plant home, it may already have a small trellis that was placed in the pot (or part of the pot) for it to climb. You'll want to, very carefully, disentangle the tender branches and tendrils so you can plant it close to its new climbing structure.

There are different types of vining plants, and how they grow their way up your structure will depend on certain characteristics of the plant, such as whether the branches wrap around the arbor, or tendrils hold it up, etc.

Some plants, once planted at the base of the structure, just know what to do. Others might need a little help.

There are lots of different ties on the market that can help train your vine—choose one that won't harm the plant.

Take the strongest branches from a point where two branches intersect and using twine or a special tie, secure them in place. Once they take, you can remove the ties.

Vining plants include:

Clematis

Climbing roses

Honeysuckle

Morning glory

Passion flower

Sweet pea

Thunbergia alata (black-eyed Susan vine)

Wisteria

Note: Don't forget veggies! You can also train food up and over an archway. Scarlet runner beans have lovely flowers, and toward the end of the season, you'll be treated with a veggie you can add to summer meals.

Clematis is a reliable climber that's easy to train up a trellis. Credit: Shutterstock

BUILD A PICKET FENCE

PROJECT FROM *BLACK + DECKER: THE COMPLETE OUTDOOR BUILDER*

TOOLS

Mason's string

Line level

Circular saw

Jigsaw

Drill

Power miter saw

Sander

2' (0.6 m) level

Hammer

Spacer

Speed square

Eye and ear
protection

Clamps

Paintbrush

Tape measure

Work gloves

Pencil

MATERIALS

Lumber (4 × 4", 2
× 4", 1 × 4" [10.2
× 10.2 cm, 5.1 ×
10.2 cm, 2.5 ×
10.2 cm])

Deck screws (2",
3½" [5.2 cm, 8.9
cm])

Finishing materials

Post caps (optional)

Galvanized or
stainless steel
finish nails

16d galvanized
common nails

Wood sealant or
primer

Finish materials

Credit: Tracey Ayton

A quaint house with a white picket fence is seen as the bucolic ideal of home ownership. In practice, an actual picket fence is a great way to create a minor boundary around a front yard. It's a look that I don't think is dated, and it also offers opportunities to create pickets or a form that highlights a more modern aesthetic.

Often, you'll see a picket fence around the yard of a corner home. I know a few people with corner lots, and it's amazing how some folks see it as a throughway they can use at their will. A small picket fence politely keeps people out, while providing a nice architectural structure around the property.

Building a custom picket fence is a relatively easy DIY project. It's easy to customize based on the look you want to achieve. And, with a little creativity, you can design your own picket shape. Building centers sell premade pickets, as well as 6 or 8' (1.8 or 2.4 m)-long prebuilt picket fence panels, if you are less interested in making your own, but still want to build your own fence.

A picket fence is generally about 3 to 4' (0.9 to 1.2 m) tall with 1 × 3" or 1 × 4" (2.5 × 7.6 cm or 2.5 × 10.2 cm) pickets. You can choose how far apart you'd like to space your fence posts and the pickets (do not exceed 6 to 8' [1.8 to 2.4 m] between posts). These can be incorporated into the fence design or be carefully hidden by the pickets.

PUTTING IT TOGETHER

1. Install and trim the posts according to how you'd like your fence spaced (see Calculating Picket Spacing, page 198).

2. Mark the stringer positions onto the posts (the stringers are the horizontal boards between posts to which you attach the pickets). These marks should represent the top edges of the two stringer boards for each fence section.

3. To install the stringers, measure between each pair of posts and cut the 2 × 4" (5.1 × 10.2 cm) stringers to fit. Drill angled pilot holes and fasten the stringers to the posts with 3½" (8.9 cm) deck screws or 16d galvanized common nails; drive one fastener into the bottom and top edges of each stringer end. Or, use metal fence hanger hardware.

4. Cut the pickets to length using a power miter saw. To save time, set up a stop block with the distance from the block to blade equal to the picket length.

5. Shape the picket ends as desired. For straight-cut designs, use a miter saw with a stop block on the right side of the blade (the first pass cuts through the picket and the block). If the shape is symmetrical, cut off one corner, then flip the board and make the second cut—no measuring or adjusting needed.

Variation: To cut pickets with decorative custom shapes, create a cardboard or hardboard template with the desired shape. Trace the shape onto each picket and make the cuts. Use a jigsaw for curved cuts. Gang several cut pieces together for final shaping with a sander.

6. Prime or seal all surfaces of the posts, stringers, and pickets; add at least one coat of finish (paint, stain, or sealer), as desired. This will help protect even the unexposed surfaces from rot.

7. Set up a string line to guide the picket installation. Clamp a mason's string to two posts at the desired height for the tops of the pickets.

Note: To help prevent rot and to make it easier to trim the grass, install the pickets at least 2" (5.1 cm) above the ground.

8. Install the pickets. Using a cleat spacer cut to the width of the picket gap, set each picket in place and drill even pairs of pilot holes into each stringer. Fasten the pickets with 2" (5.1 cm) deck screws. Check the first picket (and every few thereafter) for plumb with a level as you work.

9. Add the post caps (if using). Wood post caps (with or without metal cladding) offer an easy way to dress up plain posts while protecting the end grain from water. Install caps with galvanized or stainless steel finish nails or according to the package directions.

10. Apply the final finish coat or touch-ups to the entire fence.

CALCULATING PICKET SPACING

Calculate the precise required gap dimension and number of pickets needed for each section using the formula example.

Total space between posts: $92\frac{1}{2}$" (235 cm)

Unit size (picket width + approximate gap size): $3\frac{1}{2}$" + $1\frac{3}{4}$" = $5\frac{1}{4}$" (8.9 cm + 4.4 cm = 13.3 cm)

Number of pickets (post space ÷ unit size): $92\frac{1}{2}$" ÷ $5\frac{1}{4}$" = 17. 62 (235 cm ÷ 13.3 cm = 17.7); round down for slightly larger gaps; round up for slightly smaller gaps

---

Total picket area (number of pickets × picket width): 17 × $3\frac{1}{2}$" = $59\frac{1}{2}$" (17 × 8.9 cm = 151.3 cm)

Remaining space for gaps (post space − total picket area): $92\frac{1}{2}$" − $59\frac{1}{2}$" = 33" (235 cm − 151.1 cm = 83.9 cm)

Individual gap size (total gap space ÷ number of pickets + 1): 33" ÷ 18 = 1.83" (83.8 cm ÷ 18 = 4.6 cm)

RESOURCES AND CONTRIBUTORS

Here, you'll find the sources I turn to for information along with links to the generous group of green thumbs who contributed to this book.

BOOKS

Gardening with Emma: Grow and Have Fun by Emma Biggs and Steven Biggs

Buffalo-Style Gardens: Create a Quirky, One-of-a-Kind Private Garden with Eye-Catching Designs by Jim Charlier and Sally Cunningham

Gardening from a Hammock by Dan Cooper and Ellen Novack

Field Guide to Urban Gardening: How to Grow Plants, No Matter Where You Live by Kevin Espiritu

Niki Jabbour's Veggie Garden Remix: 224 New Plants to Shake Up Your Garden and Add Variety, Flavor, and Fun by Niki Jabbour

Grow What You Love: 12 Food Plant Families to Change Your Life by Emily Murphy

Gardener's Guide to Compact Plants: Edibles and Ornamentals for Small-Space Gardening by Jessica Walliser

Container Gardening Complete: Creative Projects for Growing Vegetables and Flowers in Small Spaces by Jessica Walliser

Raised Bed Revolution: Build It, Fill It, Plant It . . . Garden Anywhere! by yours truly

GARDENING WEBSITES AND LANDSCAPE PROFESSIONALS

Creative Garden Designs—Janet Ennamorato
www.creativegardendesigns.ca

Donna Balzer
www.donnabalzer.com

Empress of Dirt, Melissa J. Will
www.empressofdirt.net

Epic Gardening, Kevin Espiritu
www.epicgardening.com

Fern Ridge Eco Landscaping Inc., Mike Prong
www.fernridgeecolandscaping.com

Garden by Design, Karin Banerd
www.gardenbydesign.ca

Gardening Enjoyed, Ken Brown
www.gardening-enjoyed.com

Garden Therapy, Stephanie Rose
www.gardentherapy.ca

John Cullen Gardens, John Cullen
www.johncullengardens.com

McCullough's Landscape & Nursery, Nick McCullough
www.mccland.com

My Luscious Backyard, Sarah Nixon
www.mylusciousbackyard.com

Sandhill Botanicals, Spencer Hauck
www.facebook.com/sandhillbotanicals.ca

Savvy Gardening, Niki Jabbour, Jessica Walliser, and . . . me!
www.savvygardening.com

Shawn Gallaugher Design
www.instagram.com/sglandarchdesign

Sean James Consulting & Design
www.seanjames-consulting.ca

Shawna Coronado
www.shawnacoronado.com

Steven Biggs
www.stevenbiggs.ca

The Art of Doing Stuff, Karen Bertelsen
www.theartofdoingstuff.com

The New Perennialist, Tony Spencer
www.thenewperennialist.com

The Paintbox Garden, Janet Davis
www.thepaintboxgarden.com

The Tattooed Gardener, Paul Gellatly
www.facebook.com/thetattooedgardener

Three Dogs in a Garden, Jennifer Connell
www.threedogsinagarden.blogspot.com

Toronto Botanical Garden, Paul Zammit, Director of Horticulture
www.torontobotanicalgarden.ca

Venni Gardens: Landscape Design, Candy Venning
www.vennigardens.com

Wallace Gardens, Nancy Wallace
www.nancywallacegardens.com

PLANT COMPANIES AND PLANTERS
BUFCO
www.bufco.ca
designs, builds, installs, and maintains organic vegetable gardens

Bushel and Berry
www.bushelandberry.com
compact, ornamental, self-pollinating berry plants

InstantHedge
www.instanthedge.com
pre-grown hedging plants

Proven Winners
www.provenwinners.com
flowering annuals, perennials, and shrubs

Sedum Master
www.sedummaster.com
Sedum Mats

Star Roses & Plants
www.starrosesandplants.com
The Knock Out Family of Roses, Bushel and Berry, and more

Vegepod
www.vegepod.com
self-watering raised garden bed kits

HARDSCAPING AND PROJECT MATERIALS
Annie Sloan
www.anniesloan.com
Chalk Paint and Chalk Paint Lacquer

Ecoraster
www.ecoraster.com
durable, sustainable paving systems

SEED COMPANIES
Botanical Interests
www.botanicalinterests.com

Renee's Garden
www.reneesgarden.com

Wildflower Farm
www.wildflowerfarm.com

William Dam
www.damseeds.ca

BUILDERS WHOSE WORK APPEARS IN THIS BOOK
Marcel Camposilvan, P. Camposilvan & Sons Carpentry Inc.
www.pcamposilvan.com

Jamie Gilgen, Cadence Furniture
www.instagram.com/cadence_furniture

Scott McKinnon, Urban Reclaimed
www.facebook.com/UrbanReclaimedof
ScottMcKinnonCustomCarpentry

BUILDING YOUR SOIL
The Compost Council of Canada
www.compost.org

US Composting Council
www.compostingcouncil.org

ACKNOWLEDGMENTS

A project book like this does not happen without an abundant amount of support, help, knowledge, and generosity from family, friends, and colleagues.

To my husband, Rich, for enthusiastically dropping everything to weed, plan, and dig up the front yard to make those DIY projects happen! Not only am I thankful for your consistent encouragement throughout the ups and downs of this entire process, I'm so happy your creative spirit is in the book!

Much love to my family . . . my dad, Bill Nolan, for the woodworking help and behind-the-scenes work that helped make multiple projects come together; my mom, Wendy Nolan, for all the gardening help and prep; my sister, Hilary Nolan Haupt, for coming through with the perfect last-minute photoshoot location and accompanying gardening; my brother-in-law, Deon Haupt, for your woodworking expertise; and my niece, Isla, for providing much-needed escapes from words. And the Fluffy Bunny Path sign, of course.

To Donna Griffith, I am so grateful your gorgeous photography is woven through both of my books. And to Len Churchill, for your fabulous technical illustrations.

To Marcel Camposilvan and Tamara DuFour for letting me take apart your driveway to plant a sedum carpet, and Marcel for your gorgeous live-edge projects.

To Jamie Gilgen, for your woodworking brilliance. I'm so happy I was able to feature your work again.

To my Savvy Gardening partners, Niki Jabbour and Jessica Walliser, I'm forever grateful for your friendship and support in this process and outside of it!

Liz "bird by bird" Newbery. Seriously, the Anne Lamott quote you sent helped me out during a particularly stressful week and carried me through! And I still repeat it to myself occasionally, though sometimes with an expletive thrown in.

To Stephanie Rose for your much-needed encouragement and front yard connections!

To my mountain biking friends—Dirt Girls, Wild Bettys, and others—for trail time and moral support!

To Sean James, Tony Spencer, Sarah Nixon, Mike Prong, John Cullen, Marc Green, Arlene Hazzan Green, and Karin Banerd for the time you spent answering my questions and telling me about your areas of expertise.

To my local gardening colleagues, including those in GardenComm Region VII, and gardening friends I've met in the last few years: thank you for your knowledge, front yard contacts, photos, and friendship.

And to my editors, Thom O'Hearn and Mark Johanson, for your incredible patience, organization, and direction.

MEET TARA NOLAN

Credit: Jessica Waugh

Tara Nolan is a garden writer, author, editor, and speaker. She is a cofounder of the award-winning gardening website Savvy Gardening (savvygardening.com). Her garden writing has appeared in the *Globe and Mail*, the *Toronto Star*, *CBC Life*, *Reader's Digest*, *Canadian Living*, and *Garden Making*, among others.

Tara's first book, the best-selling *Raised Bed Revolution: Build it, Fill it, Plant it . . . Garden Anywhere*!, was published by Cool Springs Press in 2016. She also contributed to *Gardening Complete*, released in 2018.

Tara gives regular garden talks each year. She has spoken at Canada Blooms, Toronto Botanical Garden, Royal Botanical Garden, and at garden clubs and horticulture societies throughout her province. She was the award-winning web editor of *Canadian Gardening* magazine's website for six years, is a former senior editor of *Canadian Home Workshop* magazine, and has appeared as a gardening expert on WNED Buffalo's gardening special *Garden Wisdom*.

If she's not in the garden, tending to her raised beds, or tackling weeds to avoid the judgment of her neighbors, Tara is on her mountain bike riding local trails, hiking, or dreaming up a new project to build, sew, cross stitch, embroider, knit, or glue.

Follow Tara and her adventures in gardening online:

Savvy Gardening: savvygardening.com
Facebook.com/savvygardening
Instagram: @savvygardening

Raised Bed Revolution:
Facebook.com/raisedbedrevolution

Tara Nolan: taranolan.com
Instagram: @tara_e

INDEX

ALSO AVAILABLE

Raised Bed Revolution
978-1-59186-650-3

Container Gardening Complete
978-1-59186-682-4

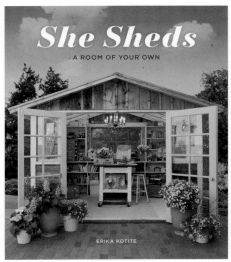

She Sheds
978-1-59186-677-0